ALSO FROM THE PUBLIC RADIO SERIES *This I Believe*

This I Believe:

The Personal Philosophies of Remarkable Men and Women

This I Believe II

This I Believe® II

MORE PERSONAL PHILOSOPHIES

OF REMARKABLE

MEN AND WOMEN

EDITED BY

Jay Allison AND Dan Gediman

WITH John Gregory AND Viki Merrick

ADDITIONAL EDITING BY

Emily Botein

Mary Jo Gediman

Ellen Silva

and the Editorial Staff of NPR News

Picador

Henry Holt and Company

New York

www.picadorusa.com
www.twitter.com/picadorusa • www.facebook.com/picadorusa
picadorbookroom.tumblr.com

Picador® is a U.S. registered trademark and is used by Henry Holt and Company
under license from Pan Books Limited.

For book club information, please visit www.facebook.com/picadorbookclub
or e-mail marketing@picadorusa.com.

This I Believe® is a registered trademark of This I Believe, Inc.

NPR, National Public Radio, All Things Considered, Morning Edition, and their logos
are registered and unregistered service marks of National Public Radio, Inc.

Designed by Meryl Sussman Levavi

The Library of Congress has cataloged the Henry Holt edition as follows:

This I believe II : more personal philosophies of remarkable men and women / edited by
Jay Allison and Dan Gediman with John Gregory and Viki Merrick; additional editing by
Emily Botein . . . [et al.].—1st ed.
    p. cm.
  ISBN 978-0-8050-8768-0 (hardcover)
  ISBN 978-1-4299-3383-4 (e-book)
  I. Belief and doubt. 2. Conduct of life. 3. Life. 4. Celebrities. I. Allison, Jay.
II. Gediman, Dan. III. Title: This I Believe 2.
  BD215.T49 2008
  170'.44—dc22

                                                              2008010110

Picador Paperback ISBN 978-0-8050-9089-5

Picador books may be purchased for educational, business, or promotional use. For
information on bulk purchases, please contact Macmillan Corporate and Premium Sales
Department at 1-800-221-7945, extension 5442, or write specialmarkets@macmillan.com.

Originally published in hardcover in 2008 by Henry Holt and Company

First Picador Edition: August 2009

10 9 8 7

Contents

Contents

CONTENTS

Contents

Contents

CONTENTS

This I Believe II

Introduction

～

JAY ALLISON

DANGLING AT THE END OF EACH ESSAY in this book is an im-
plied question: "What would *you* say?"

What would you say in five hundred words to capture a
core principle that guides your life? Can you name a belief
that underlies your actions? In the discovered truths of your
experience, what abides?

This question is more important than what one thinks
of a given essay. There are seventy-five of them here, after
all. As readers, each of us is bound to take issue with some
or be stirred by others. And your reactions won't be the
ones of the person sitting next to you; one man's cliché is

another man's revelation. Often, I find that an essay may not strike me one day, but will carry meaning months later when my own circumstances have changed.

As editors, we have aimed to be as inclusive as possible in our selection, choosing statements from teenagers to those in their nineties, and from a wide range of profession, background, and experience all over this country. You'll find writing from the famous and the unknown. Many essays arrived over the transom; some we solicited directly.

There are statements here from Nobel Prize winners, high school students, a diner waitress, an Iraq War veteran, a nun, an astronaut, a professional skateboarder, well-known artists, writers, and scientists, a drug addict, a dental technician, a former Guantánamo interrogator, and many others. Ted Gup, one of the essayists from our first collection, said of *This I Believe*, "If you take all the essays in the aggregate, what you have is a sort of national anthem. That's the beauty of it: You have a multiplicity of voices and it's a celebration of that multiplicity."

This I Believe is a snapshot of the convictions of our age. The project has spread around the globe and the response has been overwhelming. Nearly 50,000 people (that's the count at this writing; you can find them at www .thisibelieve.org) have submitted essays. Our database has been analyzed by researchers James Pennebaker and Cynthia

Chung at the University of Texas using their so-called Meaning Extraction Method, which scanned the more than seventeen million words in the essays, finding that writers used seventy-one thousand different words. Among those, they analyzed the five hundred most commonly used— excluding pronouns, articles, and prepositions—focusing on nouns and verbs. They looked for combinations and thematic links and concluded, for instance, that older people wrote more of religion, America, and the nature of existence, while younger people often wrote of financial issues, sports, and music. People in the thirty-to-fifty age bracket tended to write more about relationships. Males were more likely to reference science and sports; females, illness and marriage.

But *This I Believe* is more concerned with the individual than the aggregate. As Edward R. Murrow said in his introduction to the 1950s radio series, "In a way, our project has been an invasion of privacy, like demanding a man to let a stranger read his mail." Our team sits down every day to open these emphatically nontrivial missives, and we feel a great responsibility when we review them. My colleague Viki Merrick, with whom I edited most of these essays, said she feels like she should wash her hands before sitting down to work.

We have admiration for those who have stood up to

state their innermost thoughts. In an age of irony, an earnest statement is a target. In the newsroom environment through which these essays pass, the prevailing atmosphere is appropriately skeptical and even harsh. At its worst, it can be cynical and mocking. What advantage comes to people, particularly prominent ones, in making themselves vulnerable by speaking from the heart, standing without defense before an audience of millions? It is precisely this vulnerability that convinced us to prohibit interactive Internet commenting and discussion boards for this series. Certainly, each essay could provide great fodder, but we're not interested in the offhand dismissal or low ante insult, particularly those generated anonymously. We are interested in creating a commons, where the same contribution is expected from all: not a critique of others but a statement of one's own.

This I Believe found a natural home on public radio, because public radio was created to be a commons, a place where citizens could convene to speak and listen in the common interest. What else justifies its existence? Delivering news and music has value, but our mission calls for something more. My own work in public broadcasting over the past thirty years has centered on the encouragement of citizen involvement and finding new ways to turn listeners into participants. *This I Believe* follows in that tradition.

The primary tool of radio is the voice. Often on news

programs, the voice is used in a simple declarative way, summarizing events, giving you the level of information that programmers think you need. But the human voice has more power than that. When it is used to express personal experience, it can find its way past your defenses and sneak inside to inhabit you and even find its way to your heart. Perhaps this could be interpreted as a pitch for the audiobook of *This I Believe*, in which each of these essays is read by its writer. So be it. It is a treat to hear these stories, read in the voices of those who wrote them. Most were unaccustomed to reading their own words aloud, certainly not for an enormous distant audience. One of the pleasures for me in this project is working with the readers to get them to move backward through the page to the thoughts that inspired their words. In the voice we hear the mind behind it. The invisibility of the speaker suspends our prejudice for a moment and we can be ambushed by ideas, perhaps from those we would write off if we could see them. We don't judge by age or politics or race or face. We simply listen.

A cabdriver once said to me, while talk radio was on in the background, "Do you hear that? They're just trying to make us angry, to polarize us. No one is listening." He was right. The program was playing directly to our prejudices and our fears. Among media decision-makers, "thoughtfulness" is not the go-to programming choice for increasing audience size. Our mode tends more to cockfight than discourse. In 1951, Edward R. Murrow wrote:

> We hardly need to be reminded that we are living in an age of confusion. A lot of us have traded in our beliefs for bitterness and cynicism, or for a heavy package of despair, or even a quivering portion of hysteria. Opinions can be picked up cheap in the marketplace, while such commodities as courage and fortitude and faith are in alarmingly short supply. Around us all—now high like a distant thunderhead, now close upon us with the wet choking intimacy of a London fog—there is an enveloping cloud of fear. . . .
>
> It has become more difficult than ever to distinguish black from white, good from evil, right from wrong. What truths can a human being afford to furnish the cluttered nervous room of his mind with when he has no real idea how long a lease he has on the future. It is to try to meet the challenge of such questions that we have prepared these broadcasts.

To those in post-millennial America . . . sound familiar? We, too, are divided by fear—fear of the other, and even of our neighbor. And our media thrive by feeding it. Fifty years after Murrow wrote those words, we remain haunted by the same dilemmas, trapped between hope and fear. Our team chose to revive *This I Believe* precisely to counter the divisiveness, the anger, the prejudice, and to raise a flag for thoughtfulness.

Just as in the 1950s, our beliefs circle around the difficult, divisive questions of the age—what constitutes patriotism, the role of religion in our lives, race, poverty, immigration, America's place in the world, and the threat of planetary annihilation. And yet, we also remain focused, as you'll find in this book, on basic human beliefs that do *not* divide us, but that serve the commons: social justice, hard work, creativity, gratitude, kindness, service, a search for meaning amid the mystery of life and of death.

Many of the essayists in this book write of beliefs forged in hardship. As you will read, belief often becomes clear in the company of trauma, illness, and death. But you'll also find beliefs discovered in the calm of the everyday: serving pie, mending clothes, feeding a dog. The birth of a belief is unpredictable and unique to each individual, but the process is universal. Acquiring and naming a belief is an action in which everyone participates equally.

For that reason, our series has become popular among educators. Through these essays, young people can encounter adults thinking hard—not lecturing, but soul-searching. They hear that grown-ups don't have all the answers and, in fact, are continually looking for them, which grants young people the authority to do the same. In the Afterword and Appendices, you can read of the efforts in schools, places of worship, and other organizations to use *This I Believe* in their communities as a way to reach across the boundaries that separate all individuals, and find advice for developing your own projects.

On our Web site, after you submit your essay, we offer a space for "reflections." People often use this to tell about how difficult it was—or sometimes, how easy—to come up with the central belief and the right five hundred words. Once in a while, a writer will start his reflection with a phrase like, "What I really wanted to say was ..." and then proceed to write another essay, a better one, one that feels more authentically like the person who wrote it. There is an important lesson there for writers. And, it is important for another reason. These essays are best when the writer is compelled to write, not because he wants to give advice, but because he has something to figure out for himself. Advice, after all, is cheap. These essays are more like prayers than sermons. They do not contain counsel for others, as such. They hold, instead, the wrestling and reckoning of individuals wanting to make things clear to themselves. Some essayists tell us, "I didn't know what I wanted to say until I began to write."

In some sense, this book creates a virtual dialogue. Essayists can be imagined speaking to one another, their beliefs resonating across the pages, sometimes contradicting, sometimes confirming one another. One wonders about the conversation Tony Hawk would have with Kamaal Majeed, or Father Richard Rohr with Sister Helen Prejean, Mary Chapin Carpenter with Jimmie Dale Gilmore, or Terry Ahwal with Tamar Duke-Cohan. The Table of Contents could be a guest list for a fine dinner party. Certainly, *This I Believe* has inspired many *actual* dialogues too. I quote here with permission from Hilary Binder-Aviles, wife of essayist Quique Aviles, from a letter she wrote to another essayist in this collection, Betsy Chalmers: "Like you said, this is not the life I expected for myself or one I would recommend for others. But it's mine and I choose to live it. In the end, I think I believe that we are all connected to one another, that we are not alone, even if we never meet, that we are all part of the human experience and the most we can do is give comfort to one another. So, thank you. I found great comfort in your words."

In the first volume of *This I Believe*, I wrote that my own essay begins, "I believe in listening." That's still true, but more particularly, I believe in listening to other people's stories. This book is a chance to encounter the most important stories in the lives of some of your fellow citizens, and to understand the beliefs that arise from them. The whole collection creates a context in which to ponder your own personal philosophy. Consider it an invitation from seventy-five essayists to write one of your own.

NOTE: The *This I Believe* radio series on NPR concluded on April 26, 2009. Jay Allison and his colleague Viki Merrick have moved on to other projects, but remain in touch with many of the essayists they worked with over the years. This I Believe, Inc., is grateful to have partnered with them in this series.

Although the NPR series has ended, This I Believe will continue to collect and share the beliefs of people from around the world. Please visit our Web site, www .thisibelieve.org where you can read more than 65,000 statements of belief submitted to the project to date and contribute your own essay if you haven't already done so.

Finding the Strength to Fight Our Fears

Terry Ahwal

I BELIEVE IN FIGHTING FEAR.

When I was eleven years old and living under the Israeli occupation, I took a chance and after curfew I ran to visit my grandmother who lived two blocks away from us. On the road I had to hide under a truck to avoid soldiers who were coming my way. For twenty minutes I lay there in utter fear watching their boots walk back and forth in front of the truck. My heart was pounding so fast and loud that I was afraid one of the soldiers would hear it and I would be killed instantly.

To calm myself, I started begging God to take mercy

on me and save me from these men and their guns. I remembered the words of my mother after Israeli soldiers beat my father. She told us to put our fear and anger aside and pray for the poor soldiers, who were also afraid because they were away from their homes in Israel.

I began to feel bad for the soldiers. I wondered: Where do they sleep and are they afraid of little children like me? What kind of food do they eat? Do they have big or small families? Their voices began to remind me of my neighbors. My fear dissipated a bit as I pictured the soldiers as people I knew. Although my twenty minutes under the truck seemed like an eternity, I believe that shedding my fear literally saved my life.

Thirty-six years later I look around and see another kind of devastation created by fear. I saw the collapse of my city, Detroit, when so many white people fled the city out of fear. After 9/11, the Arab and Muslim communities segregated themselves because of the level of suspicion directed at them from others. Fear of association because of ethnicity led many to retreat within themselves and their community. They stopped socializing with non-Arab/Muslim colleagues and neighbors. Once again, we allow differences to separate us because of fear.

When I was hiding under that truck, if my terror had made me lose control and I had started to cry, the jittery soldiers might have pulled the trigger because of their own fears. Thank God I lived to wonder about this. I understood as a child that fear can be deadly.

I believe it is fear we should be fighting, not the "other." We all belong to the same human tribe; that kinship supersedes our differences. We are all soldiers patrolling the road, and we're all little children hiding under the truck.

TERRY AHWAL *was born in the West Bank city of Ramallah, and now lives with her family near Detroit. She is development director for the Rehabilitation Institute of Michigan, and teaches classes in nonviolent communication at Madonna University. Ahwal said her husband's family is Jewish and that Thanksgiving in their household is a mix of Jews and Arabs coming together with no uneasiness.*

I Will Take My Voice Back

⌒

QUIQUE AVILES

I BELIEVE THAT ADDICTION CAN KILL ME, but that writing and performing will save me.

I am a poet and an actor. I am also a crack addict and an alcoholic, and that's how a lot of people see me: a pipe head, a drunk, a problem, an epidemic, a disaster area.

I came to Washington, D.C., from El Salvador in 1980 at the age of fifteen. When I told my mom I wanted to be an actor, she said, "You mean a clown." But I make a living—although meager—through my poetry and performances.

In the early '80s, crack came to D.C. I saw my city change and me with it. Crack is a killer. Crack turns a ladybug in

your house into a hungry rat. Crack transports you into paranoid obsession. You don't sleep. You don't eat. Your high lasts
ten to fifteen seconds so you need to keep pumping your
brain with this poison over and over again.

Mine has been a life of duality. I can function on drug
street corners and at wine-sipping theater receptions. In
1995 I was part of a show at the Kennedy Center, but I was
sneaking beers into my dressing room before the show and
getting high after. I often feel a sense of pride when I put
my book and loose poems in my bag before going to do a
reading. And yet, I am also this other person—this shadow,
this vampire.

I've just turned forty-one and have finally realized that
crack will kill me if I keep on shoving it up my brain. The
alternative is death and I don't want it. I want to get old.

About a year ago, I completed my third rehab. I decided
that I would use writing and performing as a catapult for
rebound. I decided to stand onstage and share stories from
my notebooks that have borne witness to my nightmare.

1992
I want to keep playing with verbs
Write letters to old friends
And ask them to keep writing
I want to hold on to the lives of consonants and vowels

In a world of zero tolerance, talking like this about my addiction—even saying it out loud on the radio—may mean artistic suicide. But by telling my story here and onstage, I will take my voice back. People will bear witness to my life. I believe that crack can kill me, but that in the end, that communication and direct human contact will save me.

Poet QUIQUE AVILES *is the founder of Sol & Soul, a group combining art, performance, and social activism. His own work includes several one-man shows and a collection of poetry. Aviles also mentors emerging artists and helps young people find their voice.*

A Silent Night That Brought Healing

~⁓

STEVE BANKO

I'VE BEEN MOVED BY THE MAGIC OF Christmas music since the nuns in grammar school etched the words of the carols into my brain. That magic persists despite the memory of our prepubescent male voices that sounded more like a pond of bullfrogs than the Vienna Boys' Choir. The music rose above us. Even our childhood rivalries and petty differences were no match for the spell of that music. I believe that Christmas music can touch the spirit.

Those nuns taught me the music and the lyrics, but I would learn of the real magic about ten years later.

On Christmas Eve, 1968, I was a patient in a military

hospital in Yokota, Japan. My leg had been shattered by a couple of machine-gun bullets in a five-hour battle in Vietnam. My body was full of shrapnel and my hands had been badly burned. For three weeks, army doctors in Vietnam struggled to save my leg. They sent me to Japan on that Christmas Eve to give a new team of surgeons a chance to work their magic.

And I was in desperate need of magic. Somewhere it was Christmas, but it didn't feel like it to me—at least not until I heard the music piped through the PA system.

A chorus sang of "peace on earth and mercy mild" and promised "God and sinners reconciled." Another voice called to "let us all with one accord sing praises to our heavenly Lord" and another, to "sleep in heavenly peace," but heaven and peace seemed so distant to me.

My misery was interrupted by a low moan coming from the next bed. All I could see was a white cast shaped like a body; cutouts for his eyes, nose, and mouth were the only breaks in the cast. Even as the music inched me toward comfort, the reality of pain anchored me in the present. But looking at my neighbor enclosed in God-knows-what-kind-of-pain, mine didn't seem nearly as important.

The soft strains of "Silent Night" were filling the air of the ward when the nurses made final rounds with our medications. When my nurse approached, I asked her to push my bed closer to the man in the cast. I reached out and took my new friend's hand as the carol told us "all is calm, all is bright."

We spoke no words to each other. None were needed. The carol revived the message of hope and the triumph of love for me. I felt a slight tightening on my hand and for the first time that Christmas I felt I would survive my ordeal, and for the first time in a long time, I wanted to.

I believe there is magic in Christmas and the music that celebrates it, because it brings us closer together and closer to our own hearts.

STEVE BANKO *did two combat tours in Vietnam, earning the Silver Star and four Purple Hearts. In 1996 he received the Terry Anderson Courage to Come Back Award for his struggles with alcoholism and depression. Banko is a thirty-year civil servant in Buffalo, New York.*

Living with Integrity

～

Bob Barret

I believe in integrity. It's a belief that's tested in those gut-wrenching moments when conflicting values pull me in opposite directions.

Back in the early 1980s, I was in a training session for mental health workers who were volunteering to provide counseling to cancer patients who had a terminal diagnosis. Each of us was given sixteen index cards and asked to write on each the names of people, abilities, things, and values we hold dear. In the course of our imagined cancer, we had to surrender cards or somewhat abruptly have them taken from us.

At the end I had two cards: One read "Integrity" and the other read "My Family." How could I choose between these two? Such a choice was unfair and impossible. My initial thought was that I would give up my integrity, because I love my daughters and would want their comfort at my death. But then, I would realize that dying without integrity might be worse. I drifted back and forth, not wanting to choose. In the end, I uneasily kept the integrity card because I reasoned that if I lost my family, integrity would still be possible; if I lost my integrity, my life would be without value.

I ended up spending five years working with cancer patients and their families, and when the HIV crisis came in the mid-'80s I used my training to help gay men face their deaths. They did it with rare courage and integrity.

As I worked with these gay men, I began to be aware that my life was sort of a lie. When I met their caretakers and friends, I realized that I had more in common with them than with my straight male friends. For a while I tried to silence this growing awareness, reminding myself that I loved my wife and children, and that they deserved a husband and father who was respected in the community. If I began to identify as gay and claim my integrity, surely I deserved to lose my family and possibly my job and all of my friends.

As it turned out, integrity was the painful choice I

made. I suppose few of us want to hurt people we love. For me, telling my wife and later my daughters that I am gay was the hardest thing I have ever had to do. At age forty-eight, I did not know how to be gay, never mind how to find men to date. So I was alone a lot, and in those lonely days my choice haunted me.

Many times I was tempted to abandon my integrity and go back to the person my family wanted me to be. But returning seemed useless, for if I left my integrity at the door, I would not have much to offer other than my presence.

Today, at age sixty-seven, I live totally out as a gay man. To my surprise, being gay has turned out to be an opportunity for me to help sexual minorities and their families. For a while I feared I had lost my family. I think they felt betrayed and ashamed of me. But today we've found ways to live in our love—each of us true to our own integrity.

DR. BOB BARRET *is professor emeritus at the University of North Carolina at Charlotte and is a practicing psychologist. He has written about issues facing people with HIV, and the gay and lesbian experience. Barret says he is friends with his ex-wife now and that he and his three daughters have had their first family reunion with ten grandchildren so far.*

The Strange Blessing That Brought Me Home

Robin Baudier

I BELIEVE IN STRANGE BLESSINGS. I HAVE never been in such good shape. I have never spent so much time outside. I caught the last three sunsets in a row and unless I am mistaken, I will catch the one tonight. I have never felt so close to my family. I have never felt so sure that I was doing everything right.

I live in a FEMA trailer with my parents. I moved home from L.A. February before last, quitting the job it had taken me almost a year of miserable internships to get, to make sure firsthand that my family was okay. Now I work on my dad's house on the weekends and at his dental laboratory during the week. Shutting the curtain on the bunk bed area doesn't always cut it for privacy, so I spend a lot of time outside exercising the dog and just trying to get away from people. I take her out on the levee and run to get rid of all my frustration with not being able to have a job that will allow me to afford rent. I run to get out, when I have been stuck inside, reading to escape from life, not even able to sit up straight in my tiny bunk. I run to feel like I am doing something when I am overwhelmed by all the things I can't do anything about.

The reason I caught the sunset yesterday is that we have been waiting for two weeks for FEMA to come fix a leak in our plumbing. I was so frustrated with running out in a towel to turn the water off, then mopping up the floor with the rotating assortment of towels that we have hung outside the trailer, that I decided to put on my bathing suit and shampoo under the hose. But God, that was a beautiful sunset last night.

I know it might sound strange that I am indirectly describing Hurricane Katrina as a blessing, since it took my family's home and recovering from it has taken over our lives. But I love my awful life so much right now, that I find it hilarious when I am unable to convince anyone else of it.

I make less than the people working at Popeye's. I repeatedly have to suffer the indignity of telling people that I live with my parents. But I have finally gotten rid of back pain that the doctors always told me was from stress. I occasionally have weekends when I realize that I am building a house with my dad, which I used to dream about when I was six and watching Bob Vila with him. And I am back where I belong, no longer kidding myself that there is anywhere else I want to be.

I believe in strange blessings, because taking away my house brought me home.

ROBIN BAUDIER *lived in her family's FEMA trailer for ten months in 2006. Before Katrina, she worked on script development for an independent film producer in Los Angeles. Baudier helped her parents finish rebuilding their house and is living in her own apartment and working as a dental technician for her father.*

Returning to What's Natural

AMELIA BAXTER-STOLTZFUS

I BELIEVE IN SEMIPERMANENT HAIR DYE: THE kind that lets you have a few wacky purple-headed weeks in the depressing months of winter term, but leaves you plain and brunette again in time for graduation pictures. The kind that lets you be whoever you want without letting go of how you got there. The kind that lets you embrace those internal contradictions that make up an entire, oxymoronic, complex, complete human being. I believe in hypocrisy, just a little.

Semipermanent hair dye is about finding security within unlimited freedom. It's about recognizing what I have in my life and holding on to it, even if only at the base of a follicle, because I also believe in roots.

My mother always tells me that the hair color you're born with is the one that looks the best on you, and I want to make sure that there's something inside of me that's always going to be worth returning to. Maybe the house I lived in with my parents will never be home for me again. Maybe I'll fall out of touch with people I thought I was pretty close to in high school. Maybe I'll hate the way a darker brown washes me out. But I'll know that in twenty to twenty-six washes, I'll come back to something that I've had naturally forever, and I'll know it looks pretty good.

Here's where the hypocrisy comes in. Every time you get away from home, thinking how you're going to reinvent yourself, you end up hanging on to the things about yourself that are the most familiar. Feeling safe isn't about setting limits on the outside. It's about hanging on for dear life to what's on the inside, no matter how your context changes. Because, honestly, you'll never know whether you look fantastic as a redhead unless you've tried. What you will know is that you have brown to return to, when you're ready.

I've just moved into my first apartment all on my own, and New Jersey has never felt so far away. But this new independence could only come from dependence, from knowing that there are unshakable things in my life that have made me ready to face all the Big Bads in the world. We can't be toddlers or teenagers forever, and there's too much out there to experience to make me want to dwell too much in the past. So I do believe in permanent change—just not for my hair.

AMELIA BAXTER-STOLTZFUS, *an anthropology student at the University of Chicago, wrote her essay when she was still in high school in Princeton, New Jersey. Since then, her hair has been black, red, and purple in addition to her natural brown.*

The Right to Be Fully American

YASIR BILLOO

I AM AN AMERICAN AND LIKE ALMOST everyone here, I am also something else. I was raised to believe that America embraces *all* people from all faiths, but recently, that long-standing belief—along with both parts of my identity—have come under attack. And as an American Muslim of Pakistani descent, this attack is tearing me apart.

Twice, I have sworn to uphold and protect the Constitution and the laws of this nation: once when I became a citizen and once when I became an attorney. I live and work every day with the thought that this is my home. This is the place I can't wait to get back to when I go overseas. I feel the same relief many of you do standing in the customs line and just hearing English again. It is the simple relief of coming home.

But I am also a Muslim. I was born in a foreign land, my skin is not white, and I have facial hair even though it barely passes for a beard. Not only am I a Muslim when I pray my daily prayers or when I fast during the month of Ramadan, I am also a Muslim when I walk through airport security or in the mall when I accidentally leave a bag of recent purchases unattended. Every day, I have to introduce myself to new clients, judges, and other attorneys and actually think of *how* I can say my own name so that it might sound less foreign, less threatening.

When I am in Pakistan, I find myself defending America, our way of life, and our government's policies. My Pakistani cousins are quick to point the finger at America for any world problems and I push back to ask what the rest of the world has done that is so much better.

When I am in America, my beloved home, I find myself defending Islam, my beautiful religion. I tell people to envision *me* when they think of Muslims and Islam, not the terrorist mug shots they see on TV. When they can do that, I feel like an American, just like them. When they cannot, I feel like a foreigner.

The Quran teaches us that God created us from a single pair, and made us into nations and tribes so that we may know each other, not so that we may despise each other.

I am an immigrant, and I still believe in the basic right to be fully American *and* fully Muslim. But now I pray that America will keep me within its embrace.

YASIR BILLOO *speaks four languages and practices commercial litigation law in Miami. He was born in Karachi, Pakistan, raised in Los Angeles, and moved to Florida about twelve years ago.*

The Person I'm Supposed to Be

~

Andy Blowers

There's a wretched place depression drags me off to after taking control of my thoughts and feelings. It's the place where the longing for relief mutes every other desire, even the desire to wake up in the morning. There are days when I wonder if I'll lose everything: my job, my relationships, my last stitch of sanity. It feels as though I'm breathing hot black smoke.

Yet, I believe the same depressions that pin me to the mat so often also serve a bigger purpose in my life. They don't come empty-handed. I believe the purpose of suffering is to strengthen us and help us understand the suffering of others.

At sixteen, my first episode hit me hard enough to think I'd literally gone to hell. Now, at thirty-five, when I start dreaming of haunted houses and worrying uncontrollably about the future, I know another episode is looming. I've got a week's notice, maybe two. And then, it's as if I'm drifting off to exile inside myself with only a shell remaining.

It used to be that rising from the ash after the depression cleared was like resurrection. The burial over, I'd catch myself laughing or looking forward to the next day. I'd pig out at my favorite deli. But now, when I look closely, I find mental illness leaving other significant gifts in its wake, things I didn't discern when I was younger.

The discovery is like that scene from *The Matrix* when Neo finally comprehends his identity. Through the whole film, he's been beaten up by evil agents. But the fighting transforms him into a warrior. And at the right time, he understands and uses his power. He's peaceful, even when confronting an enemy. I believe my own years of struggling with depression have left me with similar gifts: inner strength and calm I can rely on, diminished fear, and compassion.

I believe the painful nights that close in on all of us in some form are the cocoons from which we might shed our weaknesses. I believe pain tells us something critical about ourselves and life: that developing strength and empathy and bravery is more essential than our personal comfort. And when I think of it like that, I'm more willing to accept suffering on its terms.

That's important because, if my pattern holds consistent, my next episode is due to arrive soon. I live with this reality but I'm no longer afraid of it. The depression has, in the end, equipped me for its next visit—and that's enough. Of course, I'll take my medicine. I'll talk to my gifted psychiatrist. But, when the dark does come, I'll stand up and breathe deeply, knowing I'm becoming the person I'm supposed to be.

Software developer ANDY BLOWERS *is studying for a graduate degree in technical management at George Mason University. He lives with his wife and their young son in Fairfax, Virginia. Blowers says, "When I look in the mirror, this is the essay looking back."*

Making It Up as I Go Along

Alice Brock

Just because you have only six plates and three glasses is no reason why you can't invite twelve people to dinner. You can drink out of a jelly jar or a tin can. And there are lots of things you can use for plates—like hubcaps lined with tin foil. I once made a steak dinner in an apartment that had only one knife. We used scissors. It was quite memorable.

I believe in improvising. It's exciting; it's an adventure, a challenge, and a chance to be creative. Not being locked into a "plan" or a prescribed way of doing something leaves room for all kinds of wonderful stuff to happen. You don't always have to follow the recipe. I always use more butter, eggs, and garlic than a recipe calls for, and the only unfortunate change this brings about is in my size.

I didn't study how to own and run a restaurant. I pretty much made it up as I went along. I was swept up with the idea—the fantasy—of having a restaurant, the chance to make something happen. It never occurred to me I couldn't do it; I only felt that way after I opened up, but by then it was too late. And of course making money at it was way down on the list of what mattered, and that allowed me the freedom to focus on creating something really wonderful.

I had no idea of how anything was "supposed" to be. I just barreled ahead, discovering all kinds of possibilities and making plenty of mistakes. And those are really great opportunities to learn. When something works, well, that's that. But when it doesn't, I have to think about why, and I have to come up with some other way that will make it work. Mistakes lead to discovery and that can produce delight, like cream of salt and pepper soup. I made it in a pinch once and believe me it's good. You should try it!

In my restaurant I rarely hired people who were trained—that wasn't important. As long as you could take down an order, treat people well, and give them an experience they would remember, I didn't care if you were dressed up as a piece of broccoli. In fact it was the oddity that brought richness to everyone.

Some have said it was too bad my restaurant was a failure. Why, because it went bankrupt? I came away richer than any restaurant owner could possibly dream of, just not in terms of money.

My belief in improvising was confirmed when I closed my last restaurant twenty-nine years ago. I just walked away. I didn't make any plans; I left everything behind and came to live in Provincetown, where I'd always wanted to live and paint. I'm still making it up as I go along.

I believe there is no one way to do things. The way that works for me is the way that works right now. But that might change tomorrow.

ALICE BROCK *was made famous by Arlo Guthrie's 1967 song "Alice's Restaurant Massacree." Her restaurant inspired the song, as well as a movie and a cookbook. Brock closed her last restaurant in 1979 and moved to Cape Cod, where she is a painter and gallery owner.*

Sticking My Nose in the World's Business

~

Brigid Daull Brockway

I BELIEVE IN STICKING MY NOSE INTO other people's business.

When I was a teenager, a man I knew killed his son and himself. On the TV news the neighbors were shocked that something like this would happen here, and they had no idea the family was in such trouble.

It was a lie. We all knew what that man did to his kids. We told ourselves it was none of our business, and now we were lying because we were complicit in a child's death. We'd seen the bruises on the children and did nothing. We'd seen the way he talked to them and said nothing. And so when the TV cameras came along, we told them we saw nothing.

I helped kill that kid, like everyone else, in the name of minding my own business.

Martin Luther King said in his "Letter from Birmingham Jail," "Injustice anywhere is a threat to justice everywhere." I'm no Martin Luther King but his call to action is as relevant now as it was then, and I know that the only way I can atone for that child's death is to butt in, even when it's unpopular, even when I'm not in the mood to fill out a police report or get screamed down by an abusive parent in the grocery store.

I've done those things, but I used to do them a lot more when I lived in the rough neighborhoods where I grew up, and when I worked at tough jobs. There was a wrong to be righted or a person to help around every corner. But then, I got a regular job. Now I live in the suburbs and work in a cubicle, and there are no great moral decisions under my nose.

The other day, I finally got around to reading the stack of bulk mail from charities that has been piling up on the kitchen table. I was confronted with countless organizations wanting me to help children who are victims of war, neglect, and abuse around the world—all of it seemed so overwhelming. And it made me want to do nothing more than just sit on the couch and watch reality TV.

But Dr. King's words keep ringing back to me. As much

as I may dislike my role as busybody, I think I'm really not nosy enough. I'm worried about saving the kids up the block, but what about kids around the world whose lives are in danger because I'm not sticking my nose in their business?

I know it's time to get off the couch and start butting in more. It begins with writing this essay, and with holding myself accountable to my ideals. I believe it's time I started sticking my nose not just in the business of my neighbors but in the business of the world. I'm not eager to be chastised for my nosiness, but I know a little boy who died because no one likes a busybody. I believe I've got no right to make others suffer for my lack of conviction.

BRIGID DAULL BROCKWAY *lives with her husband in Canton, Ohio. Before her current job as a technical writer for a company that makes computer systems for car washes, Brockway used to work in group homes for children and adults with mental illness.*

Teaching a Bad Dog New Tricks

~

David Buetow

I believe in my dog.

I believe in the way he lives his life, and I try to emulate him. I strive to gain his level of happiness in the simplest of things. Like the way he approaches each meal with endless appreciation and even joy. While I struggle to decide what to eat from full cupboards and lament what I don't have, he circles the floor, excitedly anticipating the very same meal, in the very same portion, at the very same time every day.

I believe in how he lives in the present. As my day fills with stress, crowded commutes, and endless deadlines, I think of Duncan home alone. His day was probably boring, but he's ready to move right past it once we're together.

I believe in his egalitarian treatment of everyone despite race, creed, or appearance. He never prejudges. Before I had him, I considered myself "street smart," avoiding eye contact with people I didn't know or didn't think I wanted to know. Running through Chicago neighborhoods with Duncan has changed all that. Now when people smile at us, I smile back, and if Duncan stops to say hello I stop and greet them, too.

I never had a dog before; I got Duncan at the urging of a friend who had probably grown as tired of my bachelor behavior as I had. My long work nights and weekends always ended with a lonely run, a bourbon or two, or a phone call to someone I didn't really listen to. All I talked about was me and what was wrong with my life. My friends stopped asking me out because I was always either at work or talking about work.

I had dates with women who would mistakenly think I was loyal to them but I never returned their calls or thanked them for the cookies they left on my doorstep. I was what some people would call "a dog"—a bad dog. Not one person depended on me, nor I upon them. One Sunday I woke up at noon, and I suddenly noticed how silent my house was—and my life. I realized I couldn't expect any valued relationship until I created one first. So I got Duncan.

All of a sudden, where no one depended on me, he did. It was extreme detox from selfishness: Let me out. Feed me. Clean up after me. Watch me sleep. I found that I actually liked being relied upon. When I realized that I could meet his needs, I also realized he met mine.

I believe in the nobility of Duncan's loyalty, and his enthusiasm. Every time I come in the door, he's waiting to greet me with glee.

Now, when my girlfriend comes over, I get up and run to the door to greet her like I learned to do from my dog.

Before he met his chocolate Labrador, Duncan, trial attorney DAVID BUETOW *was a lifelong bachelor. Since Buetow wrote his essay, his girlfriend became his fiancée, and they, along with Duncan, live on Chicago's North Side, where all three spend many evenings together at home.*

The Learning Curve of Gratitude

⁓

MARY CHAPIN CARPENTER

I BELIEVE IN WHAT I LEARNED AT the grocery store.

Eight weeks ago I was released from the hospital after suffering a pulmonary embolism. I had just finished a tour and a week after returning home, severe chest pain and terrible breathlessness landed me in the ER. A scan revealed blood clots in my lungs.

Everyone told me how lucky I was. A pulmonary embolism can take your life in an instant. I was familiar enough with the medical term, but not familiar with the pain, the fear, and the depression that followed.

Everything I had been looking forward to came to a

screeching halt. I had to cancel my upcoming tour. I had to let my musicians and crewmembers go. The record company, the booking agency: I felt that I had let everyone down. But there was nothing to do but get out of the hospital, go home, and get well.

I tried hard to see my unexpected time off as a gift, but I would open a novel and couldn't concentrate. I would turn on the radio, then shut it off. Familiar clouds gathered above my head, and I couldn't make them go away with a pill or a movie or a walk. This unexpected time was becoming a curse, filling me with anxiety, fear, and self-loathing—all of the ingredients of the darkness that is depression.

Sometimes, it's the smile of a stranger that helps. Sometimes it's a phone call from a long-absent friend, checking on you. I found my lifeline at the grocery store.

One morning, the young man who rang up my groceries and asked me if I wanted paper or plastic also told me to enjoy the rest of my day. I looked at him and I knew he meant it. It stopped me in my tracks. I went out and I sat in my car and cried.

What I want more than ever is to appreciate that I have this day, and tomorrow, and hopefully days beyond that. I am experiencing the learning curve of gratitude.

I don't want to say "have a nice day" like a robot. I don't

want to get mad at the elderly driver in front of me. I don't want to go crazy when my Internet access is messed up. I don't want to be jealous of someone else's success. You could say that this litany of sins indicates that I don't want to be human. The learning curve of gratitude, however, is showing me exactly how human I am.

I don't know if my doctors will ever be able to give me the precise reason why I had a life-threatening illness. I do know that the young man in the grocery store reminded me that every day is all there is, and that is my belief.

Tonight I will cook dinner, tell my husband how much I love him, curl up with the dogs, watch the sun go down over the mountains, and climb into bed. I will think about how uncomplicated it all is. I will wonder at how it took me my entire life to appreciate just one day.

MARY CHAPIN CARPENTER *is a five-time Grammy Award–winning singer-songwriter. She has produced eleven albums in her twenty-year career, including* The Calling, *released in 2007. Carpenter and her husband live near Charlottesville, Virginia.*

Failure Is a Good Thing

~

Jon Carroll

LAST WEEK MY GRANDDAUGHTER STARTED KINDERGARTEN, AND, as is conventional, I wished her success. I was lying. What I actually wish for her is failure. I believe in the power of failure.

Success is boring. Success is proving that you can do something that you already know you can do, or doing something correctly the first time, which can often be a problematic victory. First-time success is usually a fluke. First-time failure, by contrast, is expected; it is the natural order of things.

Failure is how we learn. I have been told of an African

phrase describing a good cook as "she who has broken many pots." If you've spent enough time in the kitchen to have broken a lot of pots, probably you know a fair amount about cooking. I once had a late dinner with a group of chefs, and they spent time comparing knife wounds and burn scars. They knew how much credibility their failures gave them.

I earn my living by writing a daily newspaper column. Each week I am aware that one column is going to be the worst column of the week. I don't set out to write it; I try my best every day. Still, every week, one column is inferior to all the others, sometimes spectacularly so.

I have learned to cherish that column. A successful column usually means I am treading on familiar ground, going with the tricks that work, preaching to the choir, or dressing up popular sentiments in fancy words. Often in my inferior columns, I am trying to pull off something I've never done before, something I'm not even sure can be done.

My younger daughter is a trapeze artist. She spent three years putting together an act. She did it successfully for a decade with the Cirque du Soleil. There was no reason for her to change the act—but she did anyway. She said she was no longer learning anything new and she was bored; and if she was bored, there was no point in subjecting her body to all that stress. So she changed the act. She risked failure and profound public embarrassment in order to feed her soul. And if she can do that fifteen feet in the air, we all should be able to do it.

My granddaughter is a perfectionist, probably too much of one. She will feel her failures, and I will want to comfort her. But I will also, I hope, remind her of what she learned, and how she can do whatever it is better next time. I probably won't tell her that failure is a good thing, because that's not a lesson you can learn when you're five. I hope I can tell her, though, that it's not the end of the world. Indeed, with luck, it is the beginning.

JON CARROLL *started at the* San Francisco Chronicle *editing the crossword puzzle and writing TV listings. He has been a columnist for the paper since 1982. Carroll has also held editorial positions at* Rolling Stone, *the* Village Voice, *and other publications.*

The Faith That Brings Me Peace

BETSY CHALMERS

I BELIEVE IN FAITHFULNESS.

I met him when I was nineteen, married him at twenty, and we were separated when I turned twenty-two because he was arrested for, and then convicted of, a violent crime. He had failed himself, his family, his wife, and his future, but he was my husband. I was mad, sad, disappointed, and frightened, but I loved him and he needed me, so I stayed.

I stayed through weeks of trials, years in jail, and decades in prison. I have faith in the covenant of marriage and in the God we stood before when we took those vows. I have faith in my husband and his ability to grow and change and become a better man, no matter where he is, and he has. I have faith that time makes changes in all of us we cannot avoid or ignore.

I am now fifty; he is fifty-five. He is still my husband and my best friend. I see him four hours every weekend, and I talk to him on the phone twice a week for twenty minutes. I am not deceived or a martyr. I am not stupid, uneducated, or desperate. I am a wife. I work, have a mortgage, a nine-year-old car, two dogs, and bills just like everyone else. This is so close to me it is hard sometimes to realize I am only one wife of over two million people who live behind bars. I have not made many friends at the prison. I keep that part of my life separate but it's always there, always a part of every decision and choice I make.

Somewhere in here I think I'm supposed to say I believe my husband is innocent, that the system didn't work, and we're victims of whatever, but that isn't the point. How do we choose what crime is over the edge, or what sin is too great to be forgiven? Yes, I rail against popular opinions based on slanted political rhetoric. I have grieved the loss of many of the normal things others have and have done, like having children and vacations abroad.

This is not the life I would have expected for myself thirty years ago and it isn't one I would recommend to others, but it is my life. At fifty I have come to the conclusion it is not the life I have that defines me, it is the way I choose to live that life. I choose to live it being faithful. This brings me peace, this allows me to have joy, this keeps me aware of my husband. My spiritual faith has given me the foundation to live this life, not just survive it. Faith in a God who has not abandoned me; faith in a man who loves me; faith in myself.

I believe in faithfulness.

BETSY CHALMERS *works for a communications company in Richmond, Virginia, helping to produce medical and scientific journals. Chalmers is also a deacon in her church, and says she learned faithfulness from her parents, who have been married for fifty-eight years.*

The Person I Want to Bring into This World

LAURA SHIPLER CHICO

I AM PREGNANT. IN THE BRIEF MOMENTS between dramatic dashes to the bathroom and just as dramatic raids of the refrigerator, I sometimes sit and philosophize about what kind of person I would like to bring into this world.

"If we had to boil it down to three basic personality traits," I asked my husband, "what would they be?"

I thought if I could name those three qualities, I could identify my own belief about what I value most. Just three, because I figured we'd be lucky to even get those, given our limited control over whoever pops out.

"Honesty," he said, without hesitating. That was first on

my list, too. I believe when you're honest you're less likely to end up in jail. And when you're honest, you're willing to take the harder path sometimes and so you're always pushing yourself to grow. When you're honest, people trust you, and so soon you start to trust yourself. And when you can really trust yourself—well, I believe that that is the foundation for all the rest.

After a pause, I said, "Caring about other people." Honesty all on its own can be a bit harsh, but when an honest person cares about other people, that's a powerful combination. When you care about other people, you're (hopefully) not as likely to land in jail, and more likely to become a responsible world citizen. You're less likely to be mean and more likely to have deep friendships. And when you care about other people, they tend to care about you and pretty soon you start to care about you, too. Oh, and I almost forgot: When you care about other people, you are more likely to know how to really love, and how to be loved back.

Now, for the third: This was harder. This was when we started to get greedy, as though having a baby at all, and then having a healthy baby, and then having a healthy baby that grew up into an honest, caring person wasn't enough. A long list of qualities vied for our vote: industrious, adventurous, creative, smart, kind, playful, and so on. But most of the qualities could still be traced back to our first two or, if not, they seemed less fundamental somehow.

And then I remembered what my grandmother taught my father and my father taught me: "You should always be able to laugh at yourself." I believe if you can laugh at yourself, it probably means you like yourself, deep down inside, and you know that you're no better and you're no worse than anybody else. You'll probably have fun in life. And most importantly, you're more likely to forgive yourself when you're not always honest and you're not always caring.

And finally, we thought even if you *do* land in jail, at least you can laugh at your own stupidity for getting caught.

LAURA SHIPLER CHICO *works in cross-cultural communication and trauma recovery. She helped convene survivors and perpetrators of the 1994 genocide in Rwanda for intensive community reconciliation processes. Chico's first child was born in August 2007.*

The Deeper Well of Memory

Christine Cleary

I BELIEVE THAT MEMORY IS NEVER LOST, even when it seems to be, because it has more to do with the heart than the mind.

At the same time my forty-four-year-old husband, Ed, was losing his life, my mother was losing her ability to remember. As Ed's lungs filled with cancer, Mom's brain was becoming tangled in plaque. She forgot how to start the car, whether or not she had eaten, and which family members had died—including my father.

I became afraid that one day I, too, would be unable to recall my husband, not because of Alzheimer's but simply because my memory of him might fade. So, from the day of

Ed's diagnosis until his death a year later, I set out to memorize him: his crooked smile and vigorous embrace, his woodsy smell, and the way he cleared his throat when he reached the top of the stairs. I knew I'd always be able to recite his qualities—kind, gentle, smart, funny—but I wanted to be able to conjure up the physical man in my mind, as fully as possible, when he was gone.

Back then, I thought memory was a deliberate, cognitive process, like remembering multiplication tables, or lyrics, or where the keys were. Unable to rescue Ed from cancer, I was determined to save him from the only thing worse than dying: being forgotten.

Later I learned that memory has a will of its own. You can't control it any more than you can influence the weather. When it springs up, a person loved and lost is found, if only for a few seconds.

Recently when I was driving, I had a deep and sudden sense of Ed, and the way it felt to have him next to me in the car. My body softened as it used to when we were together, seven years ago, living a shared life. I wasn't remembering his face or the way he walked; the careful details I had stored had nothing to do with this moment in the car. Looking in the rearview mirror, I recognized in my own face the same look I once saw on my mother's face in the nursing home. I had asked her a question about my father, and she became confused about his identity. Yet, as she sat there, dressed in a shapeless polyester outfit, she briefly appeared young and radiant, her face filled with love and her eyes misty. Her brain couldn't label the man correctly, but that was not important. It was clear to me that her husband was vivid in her heart, a memory even Alzheimer's could not crush.

I believe there is a difference between memory and remembering. Remembering has to do with turning the oven off before leaving the house, but memory is nurtured by emotion. It springs from a deeper well, safe from dementia and the passage of time.

CHRISTINE CLEARY *is a communications manager at Dana-Farber Cancer Institute, where she helps patients and their families write about their experiences with cancer. She is also writing a book about the art and science of memory. Cleary lives in Cambridge, Massachusetts, with her two daughters.*

A Marriage That's Good Enough

~

CORINNE COLBERT

MY HUSBAND IS NOT MY BEST FRIEND. He doesn't complete me. In fact, he can be a self-absorbed jerk. We're nearly polar opposites: He's a lifetime member of the NRA who doesn't care for journalists, and I'm a lifelong liberal with a journalism degree. On the other hand, he doesn't beat or emotionally abuse me. He doesn't drink or chase other women. He's a good provider. So I'm sticking with him.

Some people would call that "settling," like it's a bad thing. But I believe in settling.

The *Random House Unabridged Dictionary* defines "to settle" as "to place in a desired state or order; to quiet, calm, or bring to rest; to make stable." In short, it means that a bird in the hand is worth two in the bush.

Alas, too many of us buy into a different adage: that the grass is greener on the other side of the fence. From movies to magazines to commercials, we're told we should demand more from lives that are, for many of us, pretty good. We're supposed to look better, eat better, find better jobs, be better lovers and parents and workers. A stable marriage isn't enough; it's supposed to be a fairy tale. Perfection is the goal.

But at what cost? Would I really be any happier if I take up yoga and eat more soy? If my spouse wasn't just my partner, but my soul mate? I doubt it.

Settling, in my sense, is about acceptance. I'm a pretty happy person, in large part because I'm honest with myself about what I have. My body isn't bikini-worthy, but it's healthy. I'll never write for *Rolling Stone* as I once dreamed, but I am making a living as a writer. I yell at my sons and let them play too much GameCube, but I'm still a good mom.

Of course, some situations are worth improving. If your weight jeopardizes your health, exercise and change your eating habits. If your job makes you truly miserable, find a new one. If your marriage is toxic, end it. Chances are, though, you probably have what you need: a roof over your head, food on the table, a job that pays the bills, and family and friends. If you're unhappy, ask yourself: Am I unhappy because I really don't have what I need, or because I just want more?

So yes, I'm settling. Sure, I wish my husband would kiss me more often, tell me he loves me every day, and get as excited about my accomplishments as I do. Emptying the dishwasher without being asked and giving me unsolicited foot massages wouldn't hurt, either.

All that would be nice, but it's not necessary. I'm happy with my husband who, despite his flaws, is a caring father, capable of acts of stunning generosity, and fiercely protective of his family. Thinking about him may not set me on fire as it used to, but after seventeen years and two kids, our love is still warm. And I believe that's good enough.

Newsletter writer CORINNE COLBERT *lives with her family in Athens, Ohio. She is also president of her local parent-teacher organization, which often finds her talking with other mothers about their expectations of themselves and their marriages.*

Creating Our Own Happiness

~

Wayne Coyne

I BELIEVE WE HAVE THE POWER TO create our own happiness. I believe the real magic in the world is done by humans. I believe normal life is extraordinary.

I was sitting in my car at a stoplight intersection, listening to the radio. I was, I guess, lost in the moment, thinking how happy I was to be inside my nice warm car. It was cold and windy outside, and I thought, "Life is good."

Now this was a long light. As I waited, I noticed two people huddled together at the bus stop. To my eyes, they looked uncomfortable; they looked cold and they looked poor. Their coats looked like they came from a thrift store.

They weren't wearing stuff from the Gap. I knew it because I'd been there.

This couple seemed to be doing their best to keep warm. They were huddled together and I thought to myself, "Oh, those poor people in that punishing wind."

But then I saw their faces. Yes, they were huddling, but they were also laughing. They looked to be sharing a good joke and, suddenly, instead of pitying them, I envied them. I thought, "Huh, what's so funny?" They didn't seem to notice the wind. They weren't worried about their clothes. They weren't looking at my car thinking, "I wish I had that."

You know how a single moment can feel like an hour? Well, in that moment, I realized I had assumed this couple needed my pity, but they didn't. I assumed things were all bad for them, but they weren't, and I understood we all have the power to make moments of happiness happen.

Now maybe that's easy for me to say. I feel lucky to have fans around the world, a house with a roof, and a wife who puts up with me. But I must say I felt this way even when I was working at Long John Silver's. I worked there for eleven years as a fry cook. When you work at a place that long, you see teenagers coming in on their first dates; then they're married; then they're bringing in their kids. You witness whole sections of people's lives.

In the beginning it seemed like a dead-end job. But at least I had a job. And frankly, it was easy. After two weeks, I knew all I needed to know, and it freed my mind. The job allowed me to dream about what my life could become. The first year I worked there, we got robbed. I lay on the floor; I thought I was going to die. I didn't think I stood a chance. But everything turned out all right. A lot of people look at life as a series of miserable tasks but after that, I didn't.

I believe this is something all of us can do: Try to be happy within the context of the life we're actually living. Happiness is not a situation to be longed for, or a convergence of lucky happenstance. Through the power of our own minds, we can help ourselves. This I believe.

WAYNE COYNE *is singer and guitarist for the Grammy Award–winning rock band The Flaming Lips. He wrote and directed* Christmas on Mars, *a science-fiction film featuring the group. Coyne and his wife, Michelle, a photographer, live in Oklahoma City.*

A Way to Honor Life

CORTNEY DAVIS

I BELIEVE IN GRIEF. ALMOST EVERY DAY, when I walk into the hospital where I work as a nurse practitioner, I hear crying, moaning, or wailing: A young woman has miscarried; an elderly widower is holding his wife's belongings; a mother stands guard over her badly burned child.

Once I would have rushed to comfort these people. Uncomfortable myself with their grief, I'd want to ease their sadness with my cheer and consolation. I'd hug a patient and tell her to "try to get pregnant next month." I would reassure the widower, telling him, "Your wife had a long life." I'd enter the burned child's room in intensive care with a smile rather than encouraging the mother to weep in my arms.

When my own mother died I was terrified, confused about how I was expected to act. Was I allowed to be the grieving daughter, or should I be the competent, grief-denying professional? I held my mother's wrist, counting her pulse as it slowed. After her last breath, I rang for the nurse. Heart pounding, I waved good-bye to my mother, her gray hair bright against the sheets, and said, "Bye Mom," in the cheery voice I'd practiced all my life. I didn't know then that I could have climbed into bed and held her; that I should have wailed when she was gone.

It wasn't until I had stayed with many dying patients and, finally, with my dying father, that I allowed myself to grieve—for my parents, for those lost patients, for all their loved ones who, as I once did, held back their tears. At my father's death I cried like a child, not caring that I made the gulping noises of unrestrained mourning. Now, years later, I know that it is both necessary and human for us to wallow, each in our own way, in grief.

I no longer comfort others with false cheer. In the hospital, where my encounters with patients are ever more distanced by sterile gloves, computer protocols, and the pressures of time, one way I can still be present is during their moments of grief. I don't encourage anyone to move on, to replace, to remarry, or put the photos or the memories away. Grief must be given its time.

I believe that both the caregivers and the cared-for should be free to scream and cry and fall to the floor—if not actually, then at least in the heart. I believe that grief, fully expressed, will change over time into something less overpowering, even granting us a new understanding, a kind of double vision that comprehends both the beauty and fragility of life at the same time.

When I grieve, when I stand by others as they grieve, even in the midst of seemingly unbearable sorrow, grief becomes a way to honor life—a way to cling to every fleeting, precious moment of joy.

CORTNEY DAVIS *is a nurse practitioner at a women's health clinic in Danbury, Connecticut. As a writer, Davis has garnered an NEA Poetry Fellowship and two Connecticut Commission on the Arts poetry grants. Her latest poetry collection is* Leopold's Maneuvers.

We Never Go Away

~

Dennis Downey

I believe in genes and a forward flow of time, and in all things visible and invisible.

Smaller than a light microscope sees, a gene is a genie . . . (is a ghost) . . . is one-half of each of us given by one-half of each parent.

And each of us comes from two parents, each of whom came from two parents, each of whom came from two parents, in an endless crisscross of streams of time and persons going backwards.

And each of us is as in our own incarnation: a soul inside a body. (For some reason.)

a fire
a flame
a soul

what we desire
(that we desire)

Lighter than the flesh, the soul is the glow of us.

The soul is the particular glow that the genes make when they make.

It's the soul that stands the body up and gets it moving forward. Every body's soul is on a journey.

And I believe we live in a solar system, that we go around a sun, (the Sun), and that the Sun is a giant ball of flame.

Fire on fire on fire.

I believe that most of the energy for everything on Earth comes from the Sun, except for the energies of the Earth itself because the Earth itself is also on fire. Inside. In the center. At its core.

We know this from volcanoes: that there is fire going on inside of the earth.

We stand on an earth that is a boiling ball of iron on fire in space spinning at its core as it circles a source of sunshine.

And each generation is short. A mutation. First we're a child, then an adult, then a parent in turn to a child, then an old person. (Hopefully.)

With change, constant change, all around us all ways through out: who wears what, who's in charge, what music sounds good.

And I believe that a book is a box because a book carries something from some one person to another and because it is used (and can be used) to carry ideas across time. Which is how ideas build up.

And each of us is not only our own lives unwinding forward, but also a part of (and in service to) the larger life of the tribe.

Which, in turn, is in service to the larger life of the species.

Which, in turn, is in service to a larger life source lost in a bath of stars that is a galaxy scattered in the hugeness of the universe.

We are not lost when we die.
We never go away.
Why would we go away?
When we're gone, we come back.

Writer DENNIS DOWNEY *hails from a large Irish Catholic family in New England. His performance talks combine history, language, culture, and technology to describe the larger world beneath our everyday lives. Downey lives with his family on Cape Cod.*

The Questions We Must Ask

TAMAR DUKE-COHAN

I BELIEVE IN ASKING HARD QUESTIONS AND arguing about them.

I grew up in Israel in the '70s with the shadows of the Holocaust. We children knew that the people with the blue numbers on their arms were survivors, forcibly tattooed by Nazis in concentration camps such as Auschwitz. In my family, too, the Holocaust left scars. My grandparents managed to escape Germany, but they left behind relatives and friends.

What beliefs do such collective memories create,

especially when mixed in with the intensity of living with war and terrorism? In my family, they created a commitment to examine the morality of our actions—a feeling that we have a duty to do the right, that is, the moral thing. Even though we agree about that, my mother and I disagree about the implementation of our commitment to moral awareness.

My mother, who lives in Israel, believes that every action we take and our treatment of every individual must stand up to moral scrutiny. In this context, the Israeli occupation of the West Bank seems to her to be absolutely immoral. She also feels the ongoing occupation is tearing apart the fabric of Israeli society. She therefore joined an organization called Machsom Watch, whose volunteer women drive to military checkpoints in the West Bank daily. They monitor the soldiers' behavior for perceived human rights abuses and advocate for Palestinians denied passage.

Although many in Israel agree with their actions, my mother and her friends have been criticized for providing support to the "enemy," and even attacked.

Unlike my mother, I don't live in Israel, nor can I view the world at such an individual level. I think the need to protect society as a whole is sometimes more important than that absolute commitment to each individual that my mother feels. Moral or not, the Israeli occupation of the West Bank is a fact of life, as is the threat of terrorism. Given this realpolitik, I support the military checkpoints, which have managed to halt suicide bombings despite their negative impact on Palestinian lives.

This is not to say that my mother doesn't believe in the greater good, nor that I am indifferent to individual rights. The question is one of balance: Does the Israeli need for security outweigh the importance of the rights of individual Palestinians? I believe it does and my mother believes it does not.

The intellectual and ideological struggle in which my mother and I are engaged has at times been painful. We have remained close, however, and have even glimpsed islands of agreement as we navigate the rapids of discord. I attribute this to our shared belief in another idea, deeply rooted in Jewish tradition. This idea, to which I alluded earlier, is that we are duty bound to confront moral dilemmas and scrutinize the implications of our actions. For me, this is the main lesson of the Holocaust. We must hotly debate the political and ethical questions posed by today's complicated world and we should sometimes disagree, avoiding the dangers of "group-think," while striving for compromise.

That's why I believe in asking hard questions and arguing about them.

TAMAR DUKE-COHAN *is a business analyst, and she teaches classes about the Holocaust at Hebrew College in Newton, Massachusetts. Although they fight when they discuss the Israeli-Palestinian conflict, Duke-Cohan and her mother continue to talk every day.*

Learning True Tolerance

❧

JOEL ENGARDIO

I WAS RAISED AS A JEHOVAH'S WITNESS. If I ever knocked on your door when you were mowing the lawn or taking a nap, please excuse me. I understand: A kid with a *Watchtower* magazine on your front porch isn't a Girl Scout with cookies, but, hey, you didn't have to sic your dog on me.

I believe how we treat the people we dislike the most and understand the least—Jehovah's Witnesses, for example—says a lot about the freedoms we value in America: religion, speech, and personal liberty. And all of these freedoms rely on one thing: tolerance.

I learned this as a kid when I went door-knocking with

my mom. We were preaching that Jehovah's kingdom was coming soon to solve the world's problems. I prayed no one from school was behind those doors. Dogs I could run from. It was hard enough being singled out as the kid who didn't celebrate Christmas or say the Pledge of Allegiance. There was little tolerance for my explanation that we only worshipped God, and that God wasn't American. There was no tolerance when I announced to my third-grade class that Santa Claus was pagan and a lie.

Still, I didn't have a bad childhood. Our Saturday morning ministry meant sacrificing my Saturday morning cartoons, but our ten o'clock coffee break was a blessing. That's when we would gather at Dunkin' Donuts, trying not to get powdered sugar on our suits and dresses, while we told stories and laughed. We always knew when you were "home but hiding."

As a teenager, I decided fitting in at school and in life was worth sacrificing some principles. So I never became a Jehovah's Witness. That was the first time I broke my mom's heart. The second time was when I told her I am gay.

Obviously I don't agree with my mom's belief that same-sex relationships are wrong. But I tolerate her religion because she has a right to her beliefs. And I like it that my mom doesn't politicize her beliefs. She's never voted for a law that discriminates against gay people, or anyone who isn't a Jehovah's Witness. Her Bible tells her to love, above all.

My belief in tolerance led to a documentary film I made about Jehovah's Witnesses, and my mom actually likes it. The message is about being open to letting people have views we don't like, so in that sense it could also be about Muslims, gay people, or NASCAR race fans. The point is the people we don't understand become less scary when we get to know them as real people. We don't have to be each other's cup of tea, but tolerance lets a variety of kettles peacefully share the stove.

I believe our capacity to tolerate both religious and personal difference is what will ultimately give us true liberty—even if it means putting up with an occasional knock on the door.

JOEL ENGARDIO *is a program strategist for the American Civil Liberties Union in San Francisco. He has written for the* New York Times, USA Today, *and other papers. His documentary about Jehovah's Witnesses, called* Knocking, *aired on PBS in 2007.*

Doing Things My Own Way

~

BELA FLECK

I BELIEVE IN FIGURING OUT MY OWN way to do things. This approach can yield great results, but it's got its negative sides.

Much of my individualist, boneheaded nature comes from my grandfather.

Opa grew up in New York's rough-and-tumble Lower East Side, didn't go to college, but owned and ran two successful businesses: a restaurant and a car wash. He figured out what he wanted to do, and how to do it, without studying a manual. He used his own creativity to solve problems as they came up.

After he died, realtors tried to sell his home. They discovered he had devised his own way of hooking up the septic system. No one could figure out how it worked, so it couldn't pass codes. But it worked, and for many years beyond his time.

Sometimes I wonder if my banjo playing would pass codes. I didn't learn to play bluegrass, classical music, or jazz in school. I took banjo lessons from some of the best, but my breakthrough moments came when I left the lesson plans. I remember seeing jazz great Chick Corea when I was seventeen. There was a moment of revelation when I realized that all the notes he was playing had to exist on my banjo. I went home and stayed up most of the night, figuring out the scales, modes, and arpeggios for myself, mapping out the banjo fingerboard in my own way.

When I perform with my own group, my map of the banjo is all I need. But when I move into more conventional jazz or classical situations, I don't always have the tools to fit in. I can barely read music. I don't thoroughly understand the conventions of each tradition and I'm not sure how to voice jazz chords—which notes to leave out, how the scales work, all the rhythmic concepts.

I heard that when George Gershwin wanted to study harmony from Ravel, he was advised against it. Ravel felt that Gershwin would obliterate the very thing that made him special by learning conventional approaches to rhythm and harmony. I'd like to think that the same is true for me, but I'm not convinced. I worry that my approach might not be built on a strong enough musical foundation.

It's this fear that allows me no rest in my musical pursuits. When I'm at work—whether it is writing, practicing, or editing and mixing CDs—I obsess. To say that I am picky is an understatement. Delegating is pretty much impossible; I can be downright controlling. I have to get everything just right. Then, one day, the intensity disappears. This usually means the project is done.

My grandfather didn't seem to worry that he was making it up as he went along, and I try not to either. I believe in living with and giving in to my obsessive side when it serves the music. I believe in doing things my own way, and I want them to last, just like my grandfather's plumbing.

BELA FLECK *got his first banjo from his grandfather the same week Fleck entered New York City's High School of Music and Art. His groundbreaking work with New Grass Revival, the Flecktones, and other groups has redefined the sound and image of the banjo.*

Dancing All the Dances as Long as I Can

ROBERT FULGHUM

I BELIEVE IN DANCING.

I believe it is in my nature to dance by virtue of the beat of my heart, the pulse of my blood, and the music in my mind. So I dance daily.

The seldom-used dining room of my house is now an often-used ballroom—an open space with a hardwood floor, stereo, and a disco ball. The CD-changer has six discs at the ready: waltz, swing, country, rock-and-roll, salsa, and tango.

Each morning when I walk through the house on the way to make coffee, I turn on the music, hit the "shuffle" button, and it's Dance Time! I dance alone to whatever is playing. It's a form of existential aerobics, a moving meditation.

Tango is a recent enthusiasm. It's a complex and difficult dance, so I'm up to three lessons a week, three nights out dancing, and I'm off to Buenos Aires for three months of immersion in tango culture.

The first time I went tango dancing I was too intimidated to get out on the floor. I remembered another time I had stayed on the sidelines, when the dancing began after a village wedding on the Greek island of Crete. The fancy footwork confused me. "Don't make a fool of yourself," I thought. "Just watch."

Reading my mind, an older woman dropped out of the dance, sat down beside me, and said, "If you join the dancing, you will feel foolish. If you do not, you will also feel foolish. So, why not dance?"

And, she said she had a secret for me. She whispered, "If you do not dance, we will know you are a fool. But if you dance, we will think well of you for trying."

Recalling her wise words, I took up the challenge of tango.

A friend asked me if my tango-mania wasn't a little ambitious. "Tango? At your age? You must be out of your mind!"

On the contrary: It's a deeply pondered decision. My passion for tango disguises a fearfulness. I fear the shrinking of life that goes with aging. I fear the boredom that comes with not learning and not taking chances. I fear the dying that goes on inside you when you leave the game of life to wait in the final checkout line.

I seek the sharp, scary pleasure that comes from beginning something new—that calls on all my resources and challenges my mind, my body, and my spirit, all at once.

My goal now is to dance all the dances as long as I can, and then to sit down contented after the last elegant tango some sweet night and pass on because there wasn't another dance left in me.

So, when people say, "Tango? At your age? Have you lost your mind?" I answer, "No, and I don't intend to."

ROBERT FULGHUM *has written seven bestsellers, including* All I Really Need to Know I Learned in Kindergarten. *A native of Waco, Texas, he was a Unitarian minister for twenty-two years and taught painting and philosophy. Fulghum lives in Seattle and Crete.*

A Reverence for All Life

MICHELLE GARDNER-QUINN

I BELIEVE IN UPHOLDING REVERENCE FOR ALL life. I believe that humanity has a responsibility to the earth and to the life that we share our experience with.

As a child, I found joy digging in the dirt, examining the miracle of life. Everything creepy-crawly was fascinating to me, and I spent countless hours in my backyard exploring what wonders lay beneath. Although some people might be repulsed by this notion, these creatures did not represent slimy pests to me. Rather, such experiences in the natural world taught me about the diversity of life that could be found in any microcosm. I felt attuned to the cycles of life, my favorite being the spring.

During these budding months, I could watch the egg sacs of praying mantises as they opened or collect robin-blue eggshells that had fallen from the nests. This was where I felt a strong connection to the natural cycles of creation. This connection has inspired awe in me that I feel strongly to this day. It is a feeling deep within me that has inspired my passions and pursuits as an environmentalist.

As I grew older, I discovered that this reverence for life was not shared by all of humanity. Rather than respecting the natural world as a community of life, the environment has been valued in terms of the resources that could be exploited. Industrialization has turned life into an industry and system-atically destroys the essential diversity that provides richness to the human experience. Our self-inflicted ecological crisis has reached such a point that we no longer endanger isolated bioregions. So many toxins have been spewed into the atmos-phere as a result of our industrial greed that the climate of our planet is changing at an alarming rate. Climate change threatens all life forms by altering fundamental natural cycles, giving little time for evolutionary responses.

These detrimental impacts are visible today as polar bears lose their habitat of sea ice, the sex of sea turtle eggs is skewed, whales have less krill to feed on, and coral reefs are bleached, to cite just a few examples. Climate change also has a detrimental impact on cultures and humanity's well-being as more people are becoming environmental refugees. Little is being done to curb this crisis and, within our lifetime, the ecological functioning of planet Earth will be forever altered.

I believe that my connection to all life forms prevents me from sitting back and watching this catastrophe. I believe that we should understand our place in our regional ecosystems and communities, as well as pledge our allegiance to the Earth as a whole. I believe that all creatures, whether they are found in my backyard or halfway around the globe, should not suffer as a result of human greed. The reality of climate change is here and now; it is the environmental battle of our generation and generations to come. In honor of all life, I am dedicating myself to preventing this worldwide ecological crisis.

MICHELLE GARDNER-QUINN *wrote this essay for her environmental studies class at the University of Vermont. Two days after completing her assignment in October 2006, she was abducted and murdered. Michelle's Earth Foundation was created in her honor, and her essay was featured at Live Earth concerts in July 2007.*

A Feeling of Wildness

David Gessner

I BELIEVE IN WILDNESS, BOTH IN THE natural world and within each of us.

As a nature writer, I have traveled all over the world to experience the wild, but some of my own wildest moments have been closer to home, on the same domestic Cape Cod beach I've returned to all my life. In summer this beach is covered with kids, umbrellas, and beach balls, but in the winter the cold clears it of people and its character changes. From the rocks at the end of this beach, I once watched hundreds of snow-white gannets dive from high in the air and plunge into the cold winter ocean like living javelins.

Then, as the birds dove down, I suddenly saw something dive up: a humpback whale breaching through the same fish the gannets were diving for.

"In wildness is the preservation of the world," wrote Thoreau, but people often get the quote wrong and use "wilderness" instead. While wilderness might be untrammeled land along the Alaskan coast, wildness can happen anywhere—in the jungle or your backyard. And it's not just a place; it's a feeling. It rises up when you least expect it.

In fact, it was while observing my own species, my own family, that I experienced the two wildest moments of my life. The first happened holding my father's hand while he died. I listened to his final breaths, gasping and fish-like, and I gripped his hand tight enough to feel the last pulsings of his heart. Something rose up in me that day, something deep, animal, unexpected, something that I didn't experience again until nine years later, when my daughter Hadley was born.

Before Hadley's birth everyone warned me that my life was about to change, the implication being that it would become tamer. But there was nothing tame about that indelible moment, during the C-section, when the doctor reached into my wife, and a bloody head appeared, straight up, followed by Hadley's full emergence and a wild squall of life as her little arms rose over her head in victory. And it was somewhere around then that I felt the great rush come surging up. Sure it was physiological—goose bumps and tingling—but it was also more than that: a wild gushing, both a loss and then a return to self.

I believe that these moments of death and life give us a reconnection to our primal selves, a reminder that there is something wilder lurking below the everyday, and that, having tasted this wildness, we return to our ordinary lives both changed and charged. So, while I'll continue to seek out wild places, I know I don't need to travel to the Amazon or Everest to experience the ineffable. It is here on Cape Cod, on the domestic beach where I first walked holding my mother's hand, and where I later spread my father's ashes, that I learned that my wildest moments are often closest to home. And it is where I now bring my daughter Hadley for our daily walk, secretly hoping that the wild will rise up in her when she least expects it.

Nature writer DAVID GESSNER *is the author of six books, and his essays have appeared in* Orion, The Harvard Review, *and other journals. He teaches creative nonfiction at the University of North Carolina at Wilmington, and he is writing a novel about Cape Cod.*

All the Joy the World Contains

~

Jimmie Dale Gilmore

The question of belief has always been a source of confusion for me. Most of my life I have been torn between a deep longing for certainty and an equally deep skepticism. At times the ability to convince myself of vast, unprovable notions was kind of soothing, but the relief was usually short-lived. The truce with pessimism-bordering-on-nihilism was a very tenuous one. My outer life mirrored this conflict as I went from one extreme to another—sometimes aspiring to mystical otherworldliness and other times living in the nightlife music world not far removed from the criminal.

I did my best to cultivate belief but could only come up with what Alan Watts once called a "belief in belief." The real thing remained elusive. Brief glimpses of beautiful, inspirational meaning would slowly fade into boredom, or sorrow at the state of the world, and even cynicism. It came as a great shock to discover that my real spiritual problem was not a product of the world's condition but of my own self-centeredness.

I caused hurt and sorrow to those closest to me by living my life with my own gratification as the guiding principle. The old cliché that experience is the best teacher proved itself to me with a vengeance. For some of us, it seems, experience is the only teacher. I had to learn the hard way.

I went through a few years of just getting lost and more lost. The drugs, the sex, the alcohol: It sounds like a lot of fun—that is, if you don't figure in the remorseful hangovers, the depression, or the loneliness that is both the cause and the effect of the whole vicious circle. I went far enough down to have to either change or die. I basically managed to break my own heart.

But people are capable of learning, and learning that I had no wisdom on my own finally opened the way for me to learn from those who did. I was given a second chance. I found that what I once considered empty platitudes are actually descriptions of fact. Jesus said, "It is better to give than to receive." I now know that to be the case, not by faith but by experience. I finally discovered the beautiful, paradoxical truth that genuine concern for the welfare of others is the gateway to the only real satisfaction for myself. I cannot claim to consistently live up to this ideal, but it is with genuine gratitude that I can say I have come to believe the words of the Indian philosopher-poet Shantideva:

> All the joy the world contains
> Has come through wishing happiness for others.
> All the misery the world contains
> Has come through wanting pleasure for oneself.

JIMMIE DALE GILMORE, *known for his unlikely blend of Eastern mysticism with the deep country sound of west Texas, counts honky-tonk country, early rock, and shape note singing among his musical influences. Raised in Lubbock, Texas, he studied metaphysics at an ashram, and now lives in Austin. Gilmore's discography includes seven solo albums.*

As I Grow Old

~

DAVID GREENBERGER

I BELIEVE IN LEARNING ABOUT GROWING OLD by meeting people who are already old.

Thirty years ago, visiting my grandmother, I met a man named Herb Feitler. He and I spent the better part of a day together, going to flea markets and into the desert communities around Palm Springs. I was in my early twenties, and driving around with this eighty-year-old guy at the wheel of his enormous Oldsmobile seemed to me like the height of exotica. Later I realized what made the experience so novel: He was the first old person I'd spent time with who wasn't in my family.

In the late 1970s I worked at a small nursing home. Most of the residents were at least three times my age. Now, nearly thirty years later, I never encounter anyone even twice my age. But I continue to meet and befriend elderly people.

It's a mistake to think that old people have special secrets to impart, or pearls of wisdom to hand out. Pearls are a rare commodity and you have to work to find them. The most valuable thing for me has been getting to my elderly friends in the moment—wherever the conversations may lead—rather than through often-told stories from their past. Tales of events before my birth won't necessarily help me know someone better.

That's part of the wonder of relationships: Anything that happened before we knew each other is slightly mysterious. It's only the present we can know. And a conversation in the present is given shape by the lifetime of events and ideas that preceded it. There's no need to go fishing for the past; it will make itself known.

When he was in his sixties, after my father suffered a stroke, he started going to an adult day center. Instead of being around people who viewed what had befallen him as tragic, he met a new group of people who didn't know him before. They understood that the way he was now—needing assistance when he walked, speaking softly—was not the way he had always been. But they simply accepted him as he was. This was liberating for him. Even though his range of movement was smaller and his voice far quieter than it had been, his health was bolstered by these new relationships.

As I grow old I know issues that were once of great concern to me won't seem important anymore. I believe that having something new happen, no matter how small, is what makes for a healthy day, no matter how many days may be left.

DAVID GREENBERGER's self-published magazine, The Duplex Planet, has evolved into a collection of books, lectures, and CDs exploring his interviews with the elderly. Greenberger has a BFA from the Massachusetts College of Art, and he lives in upstate New York.

Untold Stories of Kindness

~

Ernesto Haibi

MY TIME IN IRAQ SHOWED ME THE truth of my beliefs. I believe in mankind: not gods, not devils, not angels, and not spirits. I saw man's bravery from both soldier and civilian, and I saw horror and destruction from them, too. I saw hate and loathing from all sides, and I saw caring for children, rebuilding of hospitals and schools, and feeding the poor. Not by a government but by individuals, by one man helping another man.

As a medic, I went to local clinics to inspect conditions and help when I could. I delivered supplies to schools and relief centers, and Iraqis who knew us would bring us tea and cigarettes. Language was the only barrier but a friendly smile bulldozed that wall.

I saw men moved by the death of innocents and was with those same men when they killed those responsible. On June 24, 2004, insurgents detonated several car bombs around the city of Mosul, killing over one hundred—no cops, no Iraqi national guardsmen, no Americans—all innocent civilians. Cars were covered in blood as if they'd been hit with a paint sprayer. My unit fought Zarqawi-backed insurgents in a firefight that lasted almost eight hours. Then, people moved quickly to help out—Iraqi civilians as well as American troops. But it shouldn't take a war for people to get along.

I don't justify our reasons for this war—that's not a soldier's luxury—and I don't justify what the insurgents have done to the Iraqis. But the passion of all sides—Iraqi, American, ally, and insurgent—shows that if man can redirect his energies to one of acceptance and not intolerance, we can bring the zealot, the politician, the soldier, and the outsider to a place where man is just that: man.

Many say that I'm cut off from the real world, but I believe they are the ones missing the truth. For all the death and destruction reported in the news, there are thousands of stories of kindness and caring that no one ever knows.

I believe that by striving for a world that accepts its

oneness, we can transform wars, intolerance, religious per-secution, and political extremism into memory and maybe even folklore.

SERGEANT ERNESTO HAIBI *is a medic formerly assigned to the 23rd Infantry Battalion. His military service includes five years in the U.S. Air Force and ten years in the National Guard. Haibi's blog, Candle in the Dark, explores his wartime experiences.*

Peace Begins with One Person

~

IVORY HARLOW

I SERVE COFFEE AT A COUNTER-STYLE DINER in Texas. I often see a look of isolation in my customers' eyes. They come in the front door, wander to the counter, pick up the menu, and look around the diner for something they can't short-order: a connection.

In an age of online chat, online shopping, and even online school, it's no wonder people come into the diner starving for human connection. Most of my customers can remember a time when the milkman came to their front door. As I serve up their eggs and bacon, they offer updates on their grandchildren. They ask me about the happenings in my life.

One day, I walked to the back of the smoking section to pass around a fresh pot of coffee. There was a woman who had been sitting in a corner booth for at least three hours. She asked me, "How much is just one breakfast taco?" I told her I didn't know, that I'd never served just one by itself. Going back to the kitchen I thought about her rotted teeth and tired eyes, and how she'd consumed enough caffeine for three people already. I offered her a free pancake breakfast. I fibbed that it was a leftover from an order I had messed up. She asked to borrow bus fare and promised to return and pay me back. I handed over tip money from my apron pocket. She smiled a ragged grin on her way out the front door.

Three weeks later she returned my two dollars. She had gotten a job and a friend's couch to sleep on. She offered to buy *me* breakfast on my break!

This kind of thing gets me wondering if something as simple as a short stack of pancakes can bring about a small shift in society. I'll go even further: Can one act of friendliness start to generate peace? I believe it can. Peace begins with one person but spreads like warmed syrup. When I connect with my neighbors, they return it in kind.

So I believe in friendliness and an open ear. For me, it starts with making eye contact when I pour coffee and ask my customers, "How you doing?" and then *listen* to their answer.

My job is to take care of customers at the counter in a small Texas diner, but I also believe we're in this world to take care of each other.

IVORY HARLOW *began working as a waitress after a tour of duty in the U.S. Air Force. She is studying for a bachelor's degree in business administration. Harlow lives in San Antonio with her husband and dog, and she enjoys writing poems and nonfiction.*

Do What You Love

~

Tony Hawk

I BELIEVE THAT PEOPLE SHOULD TAKE PRIDE in what they do, even if it is scorned or misunderstood by the public at large.

I have been a professional skateboarder for twenty-four years. For much of that time, the activity that paid my rent and gave me my greatest joy was tagged with many labels, most of which were ugly. It was a kids' fad, a waste of time, a dangerous pursuit, a crime.

When I was about seventeen, three years after I turned pro, my high school "careers" teacher scolded me in front of the entire class about jumping ahead in my workbook. He told me that I would never make it in the workplace if I didn't follow directions explicitly. He said I'd never make a living as a skateboarder, so it seemed to *him* that my future was bleak.

Even during those dark years, I never stopped riding my skateboard and never stopped progressing as a skater. There have been many, many times when I've been frustrated because I can't land a maneuver. I've come to realize that the only way to master something is to keep at it—despite the bloody knees, despite the twisted ankles, despite the mocking crowds.

Skateboarding has gained mainstream recognition in recent years, but it still has negative stereotypes. The pro skaters I know are responsible members of society. Many of them are fathers, homeowners, world travelers, and successful entrepreneurs. Their hairdos and tattoos are simply part of our culture, even when they raise eyebrows during PTA meetings.

So here I am, thirty-eight years old, a husband and father of three, with a lengthy list of responsibilities and obligations. And although I have many job titles—CEO, Executive Producer, Senior Consultant, Foundation Chairman, Bad Actor—the one I am most proud of is Professional Skateboarder. It's the one I write on surveys and customs forms, even though I often end up in a secondary security checkpoint.

My youngest son's preschool class was recently asked

what their dads do for work. The responses were things like, "My dad sells money" and "My dad figures stuff out." My son said, "I've never seen my dad do work."

It's true. Skateboarding doesn't seem like real work, but I'm proud of what I do. My parents never once questioned the practicality behind my passion, even when I had to scrape together gas money and regarded dinner at Taco Bell as a big night out.

I hope to pass on the same lesson to my children someday. Find the thing you love. My oldest son is an avid skater and he's really gifted for a thirteen-year-old, but there's a lot of pressure on him. He used to skate for endorsements, but now he brushes all that stuff aside. He just skates for fun and that's good enough for me.

You might not make it to the top, but if you are doing what you love, there is much more happiness there than being rich or famous.

TONY HAWK *got his first skateboard when he was nine years old. Five years later, he turned pro. Hawk's autobiography and video games have been bestsellers, while his foundation has funded skate-park construction in low-income communities across America.*

Combating the Tyranny of the Positive Attitude

BARBARA HELD

MANY AMERICANS INSIST THAT EVERYONE HAVE A positive attitude, even when the going gets rough. From the self-help bookshelves to the Complaint-Free World movement, the power of positive thinking is touted now more than ever as the way to be happy, healthy, wealthy, and wise. The problem is this demand for good cheer brings with it a one-two punch for those of us who cannot cope in that way: First you feel bad about whatever's getting you down, then you feel guilty or defective if you can't smile and look on the bright side. And I'm not even sure there always is a bright side to look on.

I believe that there is no one right way to cope with all the pain of living. As an academic psychologist, I know that people have different temperaments, and if we are prevented from coping in our own way, be it "positive" or "negative," we function less well. As a psychotherapist, I know that sometimes a lot of what people need when faced with adversity is permission to feel crummy for a while, to realize that feeling bad is not automatically the same as being mentally ill. Some of my one-session "cures" have come from reminding people that life can be difficult, and it's okay if we're not happy all the time.

This last point first became apparent to me in 1986. I came down with the flu, accompanied by searing headaches that lasted weeks after. Eventually a neurologist told me that a strain of flu that winter had left many people with viral meningitis. He reassured me that I would make a full recovery, but I was left traumatized by the weeks of undiagnosed pain. I really thought I had a brain tumor or schizophrenia. Being a psychologist didn't help; I was an emotional wreck.

Fortunately it happened that my next-door neighbor was a brilliant psychiatrist, Aldo Llorente from Cuba. I asked him, "Aldo, am I a schizophrenic?" "Professor," he pronounced, "you are a mess, but you are not a mentally ill mess. You are just terrified."

I told Aldo that two of my friends insisted that I cheer up. I tried to be cheerful for a week, but that only increased my distress. Aldo told me, "You say to them, 'Friends, I would like to be more cheerful, but right now I am too terrified to be cheerful. So I will let you know when I am not terrified anymore.'"

The moment I delivered Aldo's message I felt better. Aldo had made it okay for me to cope in my own way, to recover at my own pace, to be my own mess of a self. That was when I began to realize that I had been tyrannized by the idea that everyone must always have a positive attitude.

Having flourished in my own authentically kvetchy way, I believe that we would be better off if we let everyone be themselves—positive, negative, or even somewhere in between.

BARBARA HELD *is a professor of psychology and social studies at Bowdoin College, and she is the author of* Stop Smiling, Start Kvetching. *Trained as a clinical psychologist, she practiced therapy for many years. Held lives with her husband on the coast of Maine.*

My Husband Will Call Me Tomorrow

~

BECKY HERZ

I BELIEVE THAT MY HUSBAND WILL CALL me tomorrow.

Tonight I'll say, "Have a great day" and "I love you" to my husband, who is eleven time zones away in Iraq. Then I'll hang up the phone. I'll fall asleep as I did last night, next to our baby daughter. We'll sleep in the guest bedroom downstairs—it's less lonely to sleep there for now.

First, I'll pet and talk to our dogs. I weaned them from sleeping with me a few months ago, but they still seem a bit disappointed when I go off to bed without them. I'll promise them a long walk tomorrow, and I'll make good.

In bed, I'll lay my hand on our daughter's chest several

times before I fall asleep, just to make sure that she is breathing. I'll curl up in two blankets: one from Guatemala, one from Peru. I'll allow these souvenirs of past travels to warm the empty space in the bed. I'll get up three times during the night to feed our baby. Each of those times I'll tell her that she has a beautiful life to look forward to. I can say this because I believe that my husband will call me tomorrow.

In the morning after my cup of coffee, I'll change diapers and move around loads of laundry. I'll pour dog food, eat cereal, get dressed, and do the dishes—all with one hand, holding our baby in the other. I'll do the shopping, pay the bills, and stop in at work to see how my employees are getting by. Every three hours I'll stop what I'm doing to feed, change, and play with our daughter. I'll make good on the promised walk with our baby strapped to my chest and a dog leash in each hand. When people say, "Looks like you have your hands full," I'll smile and acknowledge that it's true, but I make the best of it because I believe that my husband will call me tomorrow.

If there is a letter addressed to me from the military, I'll open it because I believe that my husband will call me tomorrow. If there is a knock at the door, I'll answer it, because I believe that my husband will call me tomorrow.

And when he does, I'll talk to him and tell him again

that I love him. I'll be able to hang up the phone, keeping my fear at bay, because I believe—I must believe—that my husband will call me tomorrow.

BECKY HERZ *is a recreation supervisor for neighborhood parks in Sacramento, California. At the time of this writing, her husband, David, was serving in the Army National Guard on a fourteen-month deployment to Iraq.*

The Tense Middle

~

ROALD HOFFMANN

I BELIEVE IN THE MIDDLE. EXTREMES MAY make a good story, but the middle satisfies me. Why? Perhaps because I'm a chemist.

Chemistry is substances, molecules, and their transformations. And molecules fight categorization—they are poised along several polarities. Harm and benefit is one.

Take morphine: Anyone who's had an operation knows what morphine is good for. But it's also a deadly, addictive drug. Take ozone: Up in the atmosphere, a layer of ozone protects us from the harmful ultraviolet radiation of our life-giving sun. But at sea level, ozone is produced in photo-chemical smog; it chews up tires and lungs.

Chemistry—like life—is deeply and fundamentally about change. It's about substances, say A and B, trans-forming, becoming a different substance, C and D, and coming back again. At equilibrium—the middle—all the substances are present. But we're not stuck there. We can change the middle; we can disturb the equilibrium.

Perhaps I like the middle, that *tense* middle, because of my background. I was born in 1937 in southeast Poland, now Ukraine. Our Jewish family was trapped in the destruc-tive machinery of Nazi anti-Semitism. Most of us perished: my father, three of four grandparents, and so on. My mother and I survived, hidden for the last fifteen months of the war in a schoolhouse attic by a Ukrainian teacher, Mikola Dyuk.

We were saved by the action of a good man, that schoolteacher. Sad to say, much of the Ukrainian popula-tion in the region behaved badly in those terrible times. They helped the Nazis kill us. And yet—*and yet*—some, like Dyuk, saved us at great risk to their lives.

I couldn't formulate it then, as a child, but I knew from our experience that people were not simply good or evil. They made choices. You could hide a Jewish family or you could choose not to. Every human being has the potential to go one way or the other. Understanding that there was a choice helps me live with the evil that I experienced.

Being a chemist has helped me to see plainly that things—politics, attitudes, molecules—in the middle can be changed, that we have a choice. Being a survivor, I can see that choices really matter, all part of this risky enterprise of being human.

The middle is not static—my psychological middle as well as the chemical equilibrium. I like that. Yes, of course I also want stability. But I believe that extreme positions—the things you start out with in a chemical reaction, the things you finish with (all people A bad, all people B good, no taxes at all, taxed to death)—all of these are impractical, unnatural, boring: the refuge of people who never want to change. The world is not simple, though God knows political forces on every side want to make it so. I like the tense middle, and I am grateful for a life that offers me the potential for change.

Cornell University professor ROALD HOFFMANN *won the 1981 Nobel Prize in Chemistry. After surviving the Holocaust, he and his mother immigrated to the United States in 1949. In addition to research and teaching, Hoffmann enjoys writing poetry, plays, and essays.*

Living in the Here and Now

⟋

JEFFREY HOLLENDER

SIX YEARS AGO MY YOUNGER BROTHER PETER, who was my closest friend and the only remaining member of my immediate family, ended his life. Nothing I have ever experienced, or have experienced since, has had such a powerful impact on what I believe.

'Til then life often slid by me, my mind lost in reviewing what had just happened or anticipating what was to come. The present seemed to disappear between the past and the future. The life most of us lead is short to begin with; the more we miss, the shorter it gets.

I vowed to myself that I would honor my brother's

death by being present in my own life. I found a new world opened up before me—a life of richer detail, and both wider—and wilder—promise. The autopilot I'd been running on for God knows how long finally shut off. I began to see new possibilities for thought, vision, caring, and action: to say what too often remains unsaid, to admit that often I have no idea what to do.

Being present isn't easy. On a good day, I'd say I'm conscious 1 to 2 percent of the time. The rest of the time I'm reacting. Usually those reactions are not particularly thoughtful. They're just responses, old patterns, or the repetition of what I did yesterday.

Now I try to ask questions, not give answers. This isn't easy for me to do. I'm someone with a lot of answers. I have to restrain myself. Not reacting takes a lot of work, but the more I'm able to do it, the more I feel like I'm being the person I aspire to be.

I see that my own mind can be my greatest limitation (and on bad days, it always is), or the gateway to what matters most to me—the big stuff—environmental sustainability, world peace, the end to hunger, the beginning of true social justice for all. I used to think that these possibilities were beyond our reach, impossible to hope for, silly to believe in. But if we don't believe in our own ability to make them happen, they never will.

I've found that my decision to be present, that is, filled with attention to what is, is foundational.

I often cry when I think about my brother. It's one of the few things I let myself cry about. I missed opportunities with him because I wasn't present—missed opportunities I will never have again. In some ways he was almost always fully present. He didn't know any other way to be. I don't want to miss any more of my life, any more than I already have. By being present and conscious, aware and awake, I believe that I can honor my brother, just a little bit, every day.

JEFFREY HOLLENDER *is president and CEO of Seventh Generation, a producer of environmentally safe household products. His previous ventures included adult education and audio publishing businesses. Hollender and his family live in Charlotte, Vermont.*

Inner Strength from Desperate Times

~~

Jake Hovenden

ONLY A HANDFUL OF PEOPLE KNOW THIS about me, but five years ago my father died of amyotrophic lateral sclerosis, or ALS. This is a fatal disease that literally eats away at a person's muscles until they cannot walk, talk, or even breathe. It was a life-changing experience, but I can't really say that I developed any defining beliefs from it. Rather, the whole thing just really confused me on what to believe.

But this essay is not about my experience with my father's passing. It's about my stepmother.

I believe in inner strength. It was my stepmother, Janey Hovenden, who really had the hardest time when my father was suffering from ALS. For three years she juggled work, my dad, and me with virtually no breaks, but she never gave up. Every day, right after she got home from work, she would cook dinner for us. She'd have to feed my father because ALS made it so he was incapable of feeding himself. During the nights my stepmother would stay up with my dad to make sure he wouldn't suffocate while he slept. She'd stay up and comfort him, even though she had to work early the next morning. Janey even fought past her fear of needles in order to treat my dad at home because the last thing he wanted was to lie in a hospital bed during his final days.

My dad was a proud man and didn't want people to see him when he was wasting away, but Janey went against his wishes and invited old friends over to say their final good-byes. Although he didn't want to admit it, my dad cherished every visit.

I really had not appreciated what my stepmother had done before, but looking back I realize how much she did for my dad. She kept him alive as long as she could, almost single-handedly.

Today Janey is doing well and still taking care of me, just as well as she took care of me and my dad when he was sick. Before my dad passed on he told Janey that she would have to be my father figure, and though she isn't my dad, she is the next best thing. She jokes around with me about it.

Even though I live mostly with my mom, I still get to see Janey once a week. She has helped me immensely in getting through this, and I think I help her, too. She says I remind her of Dad, and spending time with me and cooking dinner for me helps her remember.

I believe that inner strength emerges when times are desperate. I believe people sometimes refuse to give up, and they help others no matter the personal cost. My stepmother proved that to me.

JAKE HOVENDEN *lives in Fairbanks, Alaska, where he enjoys snowboarding in the winter and ultimate Frisbee during the twenty-four hours of daylight in the summer. His stepmother helped inspire Hovenden's interest in forensics, which he's considering as a career.*

Becoming a Parent Is a Gift

CHRIS HUNTINGTON

I NO LONGER BELIEVE MY WIFE AND I are going to have a baby the old-fashioned way, but I no longer think this really matters. I believe in adoption now. Four months ago, the Chinese government accepted our dossier. In the next year or two, a little girl will be born and her parents will not want her. My wife and I will fly to China to meet this girl and bring her home with us.

When I was a teenager, everyone said becoming a parent was easy—so easy, I had to be careful not to do it accidentally. I guess it's easy for a lot of other people, but not for me and my wife. I'm thirty-nine. My wife is thirty-one.

For the last two years, I've watched this woman I love inject herself with needles full of hormone syrup. She got huge bruises on each side of her waist.

Our friends would bring their kids over to visit and we'd hang up their tiny coats, hoping some magic would rub off on our hands. When it didn't, we started avoiding any place we'd see the one thing we wanted so desperately. Our own neighborhood became awkward. The woman across the street emerged in the spring with a giant belly. My wife and I stopped going to parks and matinees. Taking our clothes off became a medical procedure; we obeyed the calendar instead of each other's eyes. I'd see young couples pushing strollers in the grocery store and I'd taste jealousy like pennies in my mouth. I used to believe that becoming a parent was part of our biology. It was something everyone could do. When I couldn't make a baby, I felt a little less human.

I teach in a prison, a medium-security facility full of men. I help guys write letters when they ask. Most of the letters are to girlfriends and ex-wives. I don't see long letters to children. I feel lost opportunity all around me. I can see that becoming a parent is much more than our biology.

I now believe that becoming a parent is a gift you make to the universe and that the universe makes to you. Now, I want my family to include a little girl who looks nothing like me or my wife. Someday I'll lean across a table and cut this little girl's green beans. I'll meet her teachers. I'll see her bicycle standing in the garage. I love the idea that this girl will grow up to be a woman and *still* look nothing like me, but whenever she hears the word "dad," she'll think of me.

People think we're good or generous because we're giving a home to an orphan, and giving her a family, but the truth is she'll be giving us a family. I believe in adoption because it will make me the man I want to be: a father.

CHRIS HUNTINGTON *has worked in France and Taiwan and has taught English in the Sahara and Gabon for the Peace Corps. He lives in Indianapolis and teaches at a local prison.*

Finding Redemption Through Acceptance

⁓

INTERROGATOR

I BELIEVE IN THE POWER OF REDEMPTION.

I was an interrogator at the detention facility in Guantánamo Bay, Cuba. I don't have any torture stories to share. I think many people would be surprised at the civilized lifestyle I experienced in Guantánamo. The detainees I worked with were murderers and rapists. You never forgot for a moment that, given the chance, they'd kill you to get out. Some committed crimes so horrific that I lost sleep wondering what would happen if they were set free.

But this was not the only reason I could not sleep; I had spent eighteen months in Iraq just before my arrival in Cuba. First I served as a soldier for a year, and then returned as a civilian contractor because I felt I hadn't done enough to make a difference the first time. After the Abu Ghraib scandal broke, I left because I felt I could not make any difference anymore. Those events simply undermined all of our work.

I felt defeated and frightened and tired, and I hoped I could redeem myself by making a difference in Guantánamo. Still, I couldn't sleep. I was plagued with dreams of explosions and screaming. After being sleepless for more than forty-eight hours, I began to hallucinate. I thought people were planting bombs outside my house in Guantánamo. That was the night my roommate brought me to the hospital.

When I returned to work, I began to meet again with my clients, which is what I chose to call my detainees. We were all exhausted. Many of them came back from a war having lost friends, too. I wondered how many of them still heard screaming at night like I did.

My job was to obtain information that would help keep U.S. soldiers safe. We'd meet, play dominoes, I'd bring chocolate, and we'd talk a lot. There was one detainee,

Mustafa, who joked that I was his favorite interrogator in the world, and I joked back that he was my favorite terrorist—and he was. He'd committed murders and did things we all wished he could take back. He asked me one day, suddenly serious, "You know everything about me, but still you do not hate me. Why?"

His question stopped me cold. I said, "Everyone has done things in their past that they're not proud of. I know I have, but I also know God still expects me to love Him with all my heart, soul, mind, and strength, and to love my neighbor as myself. That means you."

Mustafa started to cry. "That's what my God says, too," he said.

Accepting Mustafa helped me accept myself again. My clients may never know this, but my year with them helped me to finally heal. My nightmares stopped.

I don't know what kind of a difference I made to the mission in Guantánamo. But I found redemption in caring for my clients, and I believe it saved my life—or at least my sanity. People say, "Hate the sin, not the sinner." This is easier said than done, but I learned that there is true freedom in accepting others unconditionally.

I believe we help to redeem each other through the power of acceptance. It is powerful to those who receive it and more powerful to those who give it.

The author of this essay is a former interrogator at the Guantánamo Bay Naval Base in Cuba, where she worked with convicted criminals and other prisoners. She heard This I Believe *on the radio during her time at Guantánamo. While her identity and the facts of her story were verified by the editors through document check and chain of command, she requested anonymity because of ongoing death threats against interrogators.*

Paying Attention to the Silver Lining

~

ANNALIESE JAKIMIDES

I'M FIFTY-SEVEN. DIVORCED AFTER TWENTY-EIGHT YEARS OF marriage, I no longer have a house. I own very little, make a marginal living, and I lost my youngest child to suicide when he was twenty-one. At my core I am grateful for it all—even my son's death. It gave me the lens through which to see everything.

I believe in a silver lining.

I will forever carry my son with me. How can a mother not? This is the only choice I had: I could either carry him as a bag of rocks or I could live a life celebrating him. Now let me be honest here: I wailed for months before I figured out how to trade the rocks for the joy, and found the silver lining thing. I'm a people person, but Arrick was really a people person. He told me once, "I talk to everyone I want to talk to."

"Everyone?" I asked incredulously.

"Well, yeah, I might miss someone I need to know."

And now, five years later, I've embraced my son's philosophy.

My daughter, on the other hand, is more cautious—she shushes me when she sees I am about to say hello to a strange woman by the subway stop. "You can't do that, Mom," she says half laughing, knowing that I now see every single encounter as filled with possibilities that can make a difference in my life; that I am more eager than ever to connect with others.

Waiting for the train, I hear strains of an Ornette Coleman tune. I smile, and drop a precious five-dollar bill into the open case. My Arrick played the saxophone. I wish I had his saxophone's soft leather traveling bag with me, so I could give it to this man in case he someday finds himself on the way to a non-street gig. I tell him that. He smiles.

Arrick couldn't figure out how to make his way, how to live out the rest of his life. I believe he wanted to. When I call up that beautiful face and those elegant cocoa-brown fingers running along the sax's keys, I am always convinced of it. The youngest of three, Arrick was the smartest, the funniest, and we all say so.

He was also the darkest, but no one ever saw him as suicide dark. The why of these choices is often not clear—actually downright murky. I still don't know what brought him to suicide. What is clear, however, is that my son continues: He continues to be part of my story, the family's story, and every day now I'm still making connections on his behalf.

And so I smile at the checker in the grocery store, discuss architecture with the homeless guy who reads every bad-weather day in the library. I tell the woman my daughter thinks I shouldn't speak to that I love her fuchsia hat with the funky feathers, and I thank the saxophone player for the fine Coleman on a subway platform in wintry New York City.

Arrick's death made me sit up and pay attention. I lingered on the edges before, playing it safe, but I'm in the game now. Arrick showed me the silver lining, and I'm showing it to everyone I meet.

ANNALIESE JAKIMIDES *makes a living as a copy editor. Her poetry, essays, and short fiction have appeared in various publications. A native of Boston, Jakimides lives in Bangor, Maine.*

There Is No Blame; There Is Only Love

⁓

A NN K ARASINSKI

Y OU DON'T EXPECT YOUR CHILD TO GROW up to be a heroin addict. From the moment of her birth, you have hopes and dreams about the future, but they never include heroin addiction. That couldn't happen to your child, because addiction is the result of a bad environment, bad parenting. There is most definitely someone or something to blame.

That's what I used to believe. But after failed rehab and long periods of separation from my heroin-addicted daughter, after years of holding my breath, waiting for another relapse, I now believe there is no blame.

After Katie admitted her addiction, I struggled to

understand how this could have happened to my daughter—a bright, beautiful, talented, and most important, loved young woman. When the initial shock wore off, I analyzed and inventoried all the whys and hows of Katie's addiction. I searched for someone or something to blame. I blamed her friends. I blamed her dad. I blamed our divorce. But mostly, I blamed myself. My desperate heart convinced me that I should have prevented Katie's addiction and that, given another chance, I could correct my mistakes.

When Katie came home from rehab, I approached each day with the zeal of a drill sergeant. I championed the twelve-step program and monitored her improvement daily as though curing heroin addiction was as simple as nursing a cold. I drove her to therapy sessions and AA meetings. I controlled everything and left nothing to chance. But in spite of my efforts, Katie didn't get better. She left my home, lost again to the powerful grip of addiction.

In the long days, weeks, and months that followed, I gathered bits and pieces of old beliefs and tried to assemble them into something whole. Sometimes I gave up, and sometimes I simply let go. Gradually, my search for blame changed to a longing for hope. I comforted myself with the only thing that still connected me to my daughter: love.

I thought about Katie every day, and I missed her. I cried and worried about her safety and whereabouts. I wrote letters I knew she'd never see. Sometimes, I woke up panicked in the middle of the night, certain that my mother's intuition was preparing me for something bad. But through it all, I loved her.

I don't know why or how my daughter became addicted to heroin. I do know that it doesn't really matter. Life goes on, and Katie is still my daughter.

Katie and I meet for breakfast on Friday mornings now. We drink coffee and talk. I don't try to heal her. I just love her. Sometimes there is pain and sorrow, but there is no blame. I believe there is only love.

ANN KARASINSKI *is a retired school psychologist, but she says her most important work has been mothering. She and her family live in Belmont, Michigan. At the time of this writing, Karasinski's daughter, Katie, has been in recovery for two years and has a sixteen-month-old son of her own.*

The Universe Is Conspiring to Help Us

KEVIN KELLY

WHEN I WAS IN MY TWENTIES, I would hitchhike to work every day. I'd walk down three blocks to Route 22 in New Jersey, stick out my thumb, and wait for a ride to work. Someone always picked me up, and I was never late. Each morning I counted on the service of ordinary commuters who had lives full of their own worries and yet, without fail, at least one of them would do something generous, as if on schedule. As I stood there with my thumb outstretched, the only question in my mind was simply, "How will the miracle happen today?"

Shortly after that job, I took my wages and split for

Asia. I've lost track of the number of generous acts aimed at me there, but they arrived as dependably as my daily hitchhiking miracle.

I have developed a belief about what happens in these moments and it goes like this: Kindness is like a breath. It can be squeezed out, or drawn in. To solicit a gift from a stranger takes a certain state of openness. If you are lost or ill, this is easy, but most days you are neither, so embracing extreme generosity takes some preparation. I learned to think of this as an exchange. During the moment the stranger offers his or her goodness, the person being aided offers degrees of humility, indebtedness, surprise, trust, delight, relief, and amusement to the stranger.

One year I rode my bicycle across America. In the evenings I'd scout houses for a likely yard to camp in. I'd ring the bell and say, "I'd like to pitch my tent tonight where I have permission. I've just eaten dinner, and I'll be gone first thing in the morning." I was never turned away, not once. And there was always more, like an invitation into their home. My job at that moment was clear: I was to relate my adventure, and in the retelling of what had happened so far, they would get to vicariously ride a bicycle across America— a thrill they secretly desired but would never do. In exchange I would get a place to camp and a dish of ice cream.

When the miracle flows, it flows both ways. With each

gift the threads of benevolence are knotted, snaring both giver and recipient. I've only slowly come to realize that good givers are those who learn to receive with grace as well. They radiate a sense of being indebted and a state of being thankful. As a matter of fact, we are all at the receiving end of a huge gift simply by being alive. Yet most of us are no good at being helpless, humble, or indebted.

As with my hitchhiking rides, the gift is an extravagant gesture you can count on. No matter how bad the weather, soiled the past, broken the heart, hellish the war, I believe all that is behind the universe is conspiring to help us—if we will humble ourselves enough to let it.

KEVIN KELLY *is senior maverick at* Wired, *the magazine he helped launch in 1993. For six years he edited and published the* Whole Earth Review. *Kelly lives in Pacifica, California, where he writes about long-term trends and social consequences of technology. This essay was adapted from a Christmas card Kelly sent to family and friends in 2007.*

We All Need Mending

~

SUSAN COOKE KITTREDGE

LIKE MOST WOMEN OF HER GENERATION, MY grandmother, whom I called Nonie, was an excellent seamstress. Born in 1879 in Galveston, Texas, she made most of her own clothes. Widowed at forty-three and forced to count every penny, she sewed her three daughters' clothes and some of their children's as well.

I can knit but I cannot sew new creations from tissue paper patterns. Whenever I try, I break out in a sweat and tear the paper. It clearly requires more patience, more math, more exactitude than I am willing or capable of giving.

Recently, though, I have come to relish the moments

when I sit down and, somewhat clumsily, repair a torn shirt, hem a skirt, patch a pair of jeans, and I realize that I believe in mending. The solace and comfort I feel when I pick up my needle and thread clearly exceeds the mere rescue of a piece of clothing. It is a time to stop, a time to quit running around trying to make figurative ends meet; it is a chance to sew actual rips together. I can't stop the war in Iraq, I can't reverse global warming, I can't solve the problems of my community or the world, but I can mend things at hand. I can darn a pair of socks.

Accomplishing small tasks, in this case saving something that might otherwise have been thrown away, is satisfying and, perhaps, even inspiring.

Mending something is different from fixing it. Fixing it suggests that evidence of the problem will disappear. I see mending as a preservation of history and a proclamation of hope. When we mend broken relationships we realize that we're better together than apart, and perhaps even stronger for the rip and the repair.

When Nonie was seventy-eight and living alone in a small apartment in New Jersey, a man smashed the window of her bedroom where she lay sleeping and raped her. It was so horrific, as any rape is, that even in our pretty open, highly verbal family, no one mentioned it. I didn't learn about it for almost five years. What I did notice, though, was that Nonie stopped sewing new clothes. All she did was to mend anything she could get her hands on as though she could somehow soothe the wound, piece back together her broken heart, soul, and body by making sure that nothing appeared unraveled or undone as she had been.

Mending doesn't say, "This never happened." It says, instead, as I believe the Christian cross does, "Something or someone was surely broken here, but with God's grace it will rise to new life." So too my old pajamas, the fence around the garden, the friendship torn by misunderstanding, a country being ripped apart by economic and social inequity, and a global divide of enormous proportions—they all need mending.

I'm starting with the pajamas.

SUSAN COOKE KITTREDGE *is senior minister at the* Old Meeting House *in East Montpelier Center, Vermont. Her father was the journalist and broadcaster Alistair Cooke, whose* Letter from America *was the longest-running radio commentary series in history.*

Telling Kids the Whole Truth

MARTHA LEATHE

SEVERAL WEEKS AGO I GOT A CALL from a good friend whose husband had just been diagnosed with prostate cancer. "Do we tell the kids?" she asked.

"Absolutely," I answered.

"Do we use the C-word?"

"Yes, I think you do," I said. "The boys deserve to know the truth, however heartbreaking it is."

Adults always insist that children be honest, but how many of us are honest with our kids, particularly about the tough stuff: death, sex, corruption, our own failings?

I believe in telling children the truth. I believe this is

vital for their understanding of the world, their confidence, and the development of their morals and values.

This does not mean kids need to be unnecessarily frightened or told more than they can handle. When our son was six, he tagged along while his older sister got her nose-ring changed. In the shop, he sifted through a big bin of brightly packaged condoms. "What are these?" he said.

"Condoms," I replied.

"What are they for?" he asked. Briefly, I explained what condoms are, precisely where you put them, and how they work.

"Oh," he said, clearly disappointed, I think, that they weren't candy. It wasn't a lot of information, but it was the truth.

Many people think they are protecting children when they spare them the truth. I disagree. I believe children possess an enviable ability to cope with and make sense of what even adults find confounding; they can accept the unacceptable in a way that astonishes me.

When we are honest with children, we also validate their intuition. If we can admit that yes, people can be mean, grandma does have a drinking problem, divorce is painful, we allow children to trust their gut. They can begin to recognize and rely on their own inner voice, which will speak to them throughout their lives.

Kids also have an uncanny sense of when something is up: They know a fake smile when they see one, they realize when we're uneasy, they can tell when we're lying.

One night I was in the car with our two oldest daughters. It was dark and cozy—the perfect time for a heart-to-heart conversation. Out of the blue, one of our kids said, "So, Mom, have you ever smoked pot?" I stalled a little, but the girls persisted. They had me and they knew it. So I told them the truth, albeit somewhat abridged. What ensued was a frank discussion about the lures and perils of drugs, well worth any discomfort. I believe my honesty was much more effective than warnings or platitudes.

Time marches on, and so do children. These same daughters are in college now; we have two other kids still at home. And while I have made plenty of mistakes as a parent, I do have clear and open relationships with each of our kids. I believe that my being truthful with our children has paid off, because I'm pretty sure that now they are honest with me.

MARTHA LEATHE *and her family live in Eliot, Maine. Much of her life has focused on education and children; she has taught every grade from first through eighth and volunteered in her local public schools. She currently serves as a school board member.*

Every Person Is Precious

~~~

ISABEL LEGARDA

I'M OFTEN ASKED WHY I CHOSE TO be an anesthesiologist. The truest answer I give is that anesthesiology is spiritual work.

The word "spiritual" can have different meanings. I think of the Latin root, *spiritus*—breath, inspiration—words that resound in both medicine and faith, words that help define my life and work.

My spirituality has evolved hand in hand with my becoming a physician. In medical school, a classmate and I once found ourselves talking not about science but about faith. We had been raised in different traditions, and he asked me, "If you could verbalize in one sentence the single most important idea at the heart of your religion, what would you say?" I imagined my religion at its origins, untouched by history. No canon of stories, traditions, rituals, no trappings. One sentence to distill everything that mattered? I paused for a second before it came to me, like a sudden breath: Every person is precious. That was the core of my faith.

But when I finished medical school and started residency, my spiritual life began to fray at the edges. I couldn't reconcile the suffering of children with the idea of a merciful God. Once, while making rounds, I unintentionally walked in on parents praying ardently at their infant daughter's hospital bed. Though I was moved, I remember wondering if it was any use. I struggled to make spiritual connections.

The moment I chose my specialty, though, I began suturing together some of those tattered edges of faith. One day, an anesthesiologist taught me how to give manual breaths—to breathe for a child while he couldn't breathe for himself. On that day, my life turned. I took on the responsibility of sustaining the life-breath of others, and slowly I opened up to Spirit once again. Now, whenever I listen to patients' breath sounds while squeezing oxygen into their lungs or intervening when their blood pressures sag, when I hold their hands or dry their tears, I find myself literally in touch with the sacred.

Perhaps for some, this degree of control creates a sense of power. For me, it is profoundly humbling. I realize that if I forget I am standing on holy ground in the O.R. and fail to approach my patients with reverence, I risk their lives.

Every person is precious: This I believe with my whole heart. Each time I keep watch over patients and protect them when they're most vulnerable, my faith comes alive. It catches breath: *Spiritus*.

DR. ISABEL LEGARDA *was born in the Philippines and moved to the United States in 1981. She is a graduate of Harvard and New York Medical College, where her favorite professor was a Franciscan priest who taught anatomy. Legarda lives with her family in Belmont, Massachusetts.*

Navigating Turbulent Waters

~~~~

Jimmy Liao

I BELIEVE IN USING THE TURBULENCE IN my life. I learned this studying fish.

My mother and father emigrated from Taiwan to New York City to raise a family. They bussed tables at a Chinese restaurant and worked double shifts for years. On Sundays, my father and I would go out with our fishing rods. I was two years old when I caught my first fish in Prospect Park with my dad. No water was off-limits: golf ponds, marble quarries, private estates. We packed a lunch and we took off. Sometimes we got in trouble, and laughed about it later when we told the stories. Our best times together were spent trying to catch a fish.

But there was another side to my father. He had a temper, and sometimes he got angry and would hit me. In those moments of uncontrolled rage he could only see things his way; he would never let me win an argument. I was held under his will, unable to break out. When I challenged him, he struck me in the face. It didn't break me, but it left me petrified, powerless, and resentful. Just the same, come Sunday, regardless of what had happened that week, we would fish together.

Years later, I followed my interest in fish to graduate school in biology. I was always a good student, but was often racked with insecurity. I didn't have much confidence. I felt it was beaten out of me. I tried to find my direction but just ended up spinning around and dissipating my energy. Then one night something wonderful happened. I was researching how fish swim in turbulent flow and discovered that they could surf on swirling eddies without using much muscle. What I suddenly realized was that obstacles could actually help you struggle less. That was what I'd needed to know for a long time.

I dove into my experiments and published them quickly, culminating in an article that made the cover of *Science* magazine, and I received my Ph.D. from Harvard in 2004. My parents took a rare day off from the restaurant and were by my side holding my hand when I stood to receive my diploma on a cloudy afternoon in June.

I believe I can get around the obstacles in my life not by fighting them, but by yielding to them and pushing off from them. It is what Taoists call Wu Wei, literally to go with the flow. Now I could take the energy of my father's violence and move through it, to surge past that turbulence. I could let my father be himself without giving up on myself. This is different from forgiveness. It's the way I choose to define the events in my life—by my response to them.

There are natural streamlines in our lives. I find by letting go I can harness the complex currents of my life to propel me forward. It was the fish my dad introduced me to that finally taught me this.

JIMMY LIAO *is a postdoctorate fellow in the neurobiology and behavior department at Cornell. His ichthyological studies have taken him to Ireland, Brazil, and Tasmania. Liao is also a professionally trained actor who enjoys bungee jumping and skydiving.*

All Beings Are Interconnected

~~~~~~~~

JAMES LONEY

I BELIEVE ALL THINGS AND ALL BEINGS are interconnected.

I saw this most clearly in the time I was a hostage—for 118 days, when the world was reduced to what could be heard and said and done, while handcuffed and chained with three other men in a cold, paint-peeling, eternally gloomy, 10-by-12-foot room. But despite being vanished off the face of the Earth, there were times the walls around us would dissolve and I could see, with perfect blue-sky clarity, that everything I needed to know about the world was immediately available to me.

One day, our captors treated us to some Pepsi. We were

very excited—more about the bottle than about the Pepsi, because it meant we could now relieve ourselves in urgent circumstances. As you might expect, it's not easy to relieve yourself in urgent circumstances when your right and left hand are handcuffed to someone else's right and left hand. Sometimes, despite our most careful efforts, we ended up with an unfortunate mess.

On a later day, after bringing us a particularly greasy lunch (fried eggplant rolled up in a tiny bit of flatbread), the captor we called Uncle needed to clean his greasy fingers. He saw a rag hanging on the back of a chair and used it to wipe his hands. He did not know that it was our Unfortunate Mess Rag, and that it had been used earlier that morning.

In that moment I saw how everything we do, even the things that seem most insignificant—cleaning up a mess or wiping our hands—affects everything and everyone else. Uncle thought he was simply rubbing some grease off his fingers, but in reality he was soiling himself in the squalor and degradation of our captivity—without him knowing it, or us intending it.

Uncle was one of our guards. With keys in one hand and gun in the other, his power over us seemed absolute but he was not free. He said so himself on one of those interminable days when we asked him if he had any news about when we would be released. He pointed glumly to his wrists as if he himself were handcuffed and said, "When you are free, I will be free."

I believe there are many ways we can hold one another captive. It might be with a gun, an army, a holy book, a law, an invisible free market hand. It doesn't matter how we do it, who we do it to, or why. There is no escaping it: We ourselves become captives whenever we hold another in captivity. Whenever we soil someone else with violence, whether through a war, poverty, racism, or neglect, we invariably soil ourselves. It is only when we turn away from dominating others that we can begin to discover what the Christian scriptures call "the glorious freedom of the children of God."

Christian peace activist JAMES LONEY was captured by Iraqi militants in Baghdad in November 2005. He and two other hostages were released four months later, while a fourth was killed. Loney lives in Toronto, where he remains active in the peace movement. (This essay was produced by Anne Penman for the Canadian Broadcasting Corporation.)

A Musician of Many Cultures

Yo-Yo Ma

I BELIEVE IN THE INFINITE VARIETY OF human expression. I grew up in three cultures: I was born in Paris; my parents were from China; and I was brought up mostly in America. When I was young this was very confusing: Everyone said that their culture was best, but I knew they couldn't all be right. I felt there was an expectation that I would choose to be Chinese or French or American. For many years I bounced among the three, trying on each but never being wholly comfortable. I hoped I wouldn't have to choose, but I didn't know what that meant and how exactly to "not choose."

However, the process of trying on each culture taught me something. As I struggled to belong, I came to understand what made each one unique. At that point, I realized that I didn't need to choose one culture to the exclusion of another, but instead I could choose from all three. The values I selected would become part of who I was, but no one culture needed to win. I could honor the cultural depth and longevity of my Chinese heritage, while feeling just as passionate about the deep artistic traditions of the French and the American commitment to opportunity and the future.

So, rather than settling on any one of the cultures in which I grew up, I now choose to explore many more cultures and find elements to love in each. Every day I make an effort to go toward what I don't understand. This wandering leads to the accidental learning that continually shapes my life.

As I work in music today, I try to implement this idea, that the music I play, like me, doesn't belong to only one culture. In recent years, I have explored many musical traditions.

Along the way, I have met musicians who share a belief in the creative power that exists at the intersection of cultures. These musicians have generously become my guides to their traditions. Thanks to them and their music I have found new meaning in my own music making.

It is extraordinary the way people, music, and cultures develop. The paths and experiences that guide them are unpredictable. Shaped by our families, neighborhoods, cultures, and countries, each of us ultimately goes through this process of incorporating what we learn with who we are and who we seek to become. As we struggle to find our individual voices, I believe we must look beyond the voice we've been assigned and find our place among the tones and timbre of human expression.

Yo-Yo Ma *created the Silk Road Project in 1998 to explore the cultural traditions of the countries along the ancient trade route through Asia. A cello player since age four, Ma has won fifteen Grammy Awards. He lives with his family in Cambridge, Massachusetts.*

Being Content with Myself

Kamaal Majeed

"Why don't you 'act black'?"

Since my middle school years, I've been asked this question more than any other. It seems to me that too many people have let society program into their brains what should be expected of me, a black person, before ever interacting with me. But I believe in being who I am, not who others want me to be.

On my first day of high school, going into math class, two of my classmates pointed and laughed at me. I initially thought my fly was open, or that something was stuck in my teeth. But as I took my seat, I heard one of the students whisper, "Why is a black person taking honors?" So my fly wasn't open. An honors-level class had simply been joined by a student whose skin was an unsettling shade of brown.

Many people think my clothes should be big enough for me to live in, or expect me to listen exclusively to "black music." In seventh grade, a group of my peers fixed their cold stares on my outfit: cargo shorts and a plain, fitting T-shirt. They called out to me, "Go get some 'gangsta' clothes, white boy."

In one of my Spanish classes, as part of a review exercise, the teacher asked me, "¿Te gusta más, la música de rap o rock?" "Do you like rap music or rock music more?" I replied, "La música de rock." The look of shock on my classmates' faces made me feel profoundly alienated.

I am now in my junior year of high school. I still take all honors courses. My wardrobe still consists solely of clothes that are appropriate to my proportions. My music library spans from rock to pop to techno, and almost everything in between. When it comes to choosing my friends, I am still color-blind. I continue to do my best work in school in order to reach my goals; and yet, when I look in the mirror, I still see skin of that same shade of brown.

My skin color has done nothing to change my personality, and my personality has done nothing to change my skin color.

I believe in being myself. I believe that I—not any stereotype—should define who I am and what actions I take in life. In high school, popularity often depends on your willingness to follow trends. And I've been told that it doesn't get much easier going into adulthood. But the only other option is to sacrifice my individuality for the satisfaction and approval of others. Sure, this can be appealing, since choosing to keep my self-respect intact has made me unpopular and disliked at times, with no end to that in sight. But others' being content with me is not nearly as important as my being content with myself.

KAMAAL MAJEED *is a high school student in Waltham, Massachusetts. In addition to his studies, he works part-time at the local public library, and enjoys studying foreign languages and writing a personal journal. Majeed hopes to pursue a career in journalism.*

Be Cool

CHRISTIAN McBRIDE

I BELIEVE PEOPLE HAVE BECOME TIGHTER, MEANER, and less tolerant than ever. I never remember people being so uncool. I don't remember people getting the third degree because they decided to wear brown shoes instead of black. If you get too close to someone on the road, they want to get out and shoot you for possibly hitting their car. What's wrong with these people?

I believe it pays to be cool. Most people in this day and age are always terribly stressed and hypersensitive to absolutely everything. They will age quickly. Cool people stay young forever.

Ten years ago, cell phones were still a luxury. People still had "land lines" for their primary phone numbers. Remember when it was okay to have dial-up? Now, people don't even bother asking for a home number anymore. Is it because we're so busy, people don't even bother being at home anymore? Or is business so important that people need to get in touch with you upon demand? Didn't people survive just fine not being contacted by their boss while having dinner with their families?

As for the Internet, it amazes me that when you walk into a Starbucks, it looks like CompUSA with all the doggone laptops with people stressing out over whatever. When people need to work on stressful work-related issues on their laptops, they go to Starbucks to drink *coffee?*

Me, on the other hand, I'm cool! Why do I know that? Because I sleep well at night, and I work with people who apparently like to work with me.

Now let me make something very, very clear: I'm not always cool. I've had my meltdowns in life. Once I had a musician in my band who was a little less than cool—he was flat-out lazy! After fifteen months of playing the same music, he never bothered to memorize it. Instead of pulling him aside and addressing the situation like a rational person would have done, I let him have it like I've never let anyone have it before. After it was over, I realized that I'd cleared the room. Everyone was so scared (or annoyed), that they just left. Well, "lazy guy" left the band and has never spoken to me ever again. I'm very sorry for that. I wish I could have that moment back, but I can't. I can only learn from that, and I try very hard not to have another meltdown, ever.

Pleasing everyone doesn't always mean saying "yes" or "that's great" or "no problem." Sometimes, you have to say the opposite but with a clear, sensible, and gracious tone. Being cool is not what you say or do, but *how* you say or do it.

So I say, "Be cool." You'll see more. You'll learn more. You'll make better decisions. You'll be happier.

Growing up in Philadelphia, CHRISTIAN MCBRIDE *learned how to play bass from his father and uncle—and how to be cool from his grandfather. McBride has played with jazz legends McCoy Tyner and Freddie Hubbard, as well as pop artists BeBe Winans and Sting.*

That Old Piece of Cloth

~

FRANK MILLER

I WAS JUST A BOY IN THE 1960s. My adolescence wasn't in-fused with the civil rights struggle, or the sexual revolution, or the Vietnam War, but with their aftermath.

My high school teachers were ex-hippies and Vietnam vets. People who protested the war, and people who served as soldiers. I was taught more about John Lennon than I was about Thomas Jefferson. Both of my parents were World War II veterans. FDR-era patriots. And I was exactly the age to rebel against them.

It all fit together rather neatly. I could never stomach the flower-child twaddle of the '60s crowd, and I was ready to believe that our flag was just an old piece of cloth and that patriotism was just some quaint relic, best left behind us.

It was all about the ideas. I schooled myself in the writings of Madison and Franklin and Adams and Jefferson. I came to love those noble, indestructible ideas. They were ideas, to my young mind, of rebellion and independence, not of idolatry.

But not that piece of old cloth. To me, that stood for unthinking patriotism. It meant about as much to me as that insipid peace sign that was everywhere I looked: just another symbol of a generation's sentimentality, of its narcissistic worship of its own past glories.

Then came that sunny September morning when airplanes crashed into towers a very few miles from my home and thousands of my neighbors were ruthlessly incinerated—reduced to ash. Now, I draw and write comic books. One thing my job involves is making up bad guys. Imagining human villainy in all its forms. Now, the real thing had shown up. The real thing murdered my neighbors. In my city. In my country. Breathing in that awful, chalky crap that filled up the lungs of every New Yorker, then coughing it right out, not knowing what I was coughing up.

For the first time in my life, I know how it feels to face an existential menace. They want us to die. All of a sudden I realize what my parents were talking about, all those years.

Patriotism, I now believe, isn't some sentimental, old conceit. It's self-preservation. I believe patriotism is central to a nation's survival. Ben Franklin said it: "If we don't all hang together, we all hang separately." Just like you have to fight to protect your friends and family, and you count on them to watch your own back. So you've got to do what you can to help your country survive. That's if you think your country is worth a damn. Warts and all.

So I've gotten rather fond of that old piece of cloth. Now, when I look at it, I see something precious. I see something perishable.

FRANK MILLER is a comic book artist whose titles include "Batman: The Dark Knight Returns" and "Sin City" (which he codirected for the movie). Miller recently announced that he's working on a new graphic novel in which Batman pits himself against terrorists.

My Home Is New Orleans

MIKE MILLER

I BELIEVE IN ATTACHMENT TO PLACE. I believe that watermarks fade, tears dry, and lives mend.

A year after the flood, the nation is remembering Hurricane Katrina. And some of us, whether labeled "displaced," "evacuated," or "back home," will wonder if we still believe. We will wonder—sitting on our porches, in our bar rooms, and in our gutted homes—if we still should believe.

When I left New Orleans, I found myself, like thousands of displaced Gulf Coast residents, living on the generosity of others. People opened their homes to me. In some ways, life was easier. I'd almost forgotten how tough it is to live in New Orleans. In Chicago I was offered jobs that pay three times more than anything I could make in New Orleans. I thought about moving: Seattle, Anchorage, New York, Key West, Tucson, and everywhere in between. But looking at a map spread on a table, I already knew. My home is New Orleans . . . still.

I moved back into an apartment uptown in the Twelfth Ward—on the third floor this time. I'm a little paranoid about flooding. But now I can really hear the foghorns of the ships on the river.

Life in New Orleans is hard nowadays. I work for the Louisiana Family Recovery Corps and I can see the mental health scene is not good: Depression is rampant. Suicides and substance abuse have been on the rise since Katrina.

I'm also back bartending and, mixed in with the grief, I can feel the pulse still there. We live the best we can. It's like this street musician in the Quarter who always says, "Man, we just trying to get back to abnormal!"

I believe the soul of this place cannot be easily destroyed by wind and rain. I believe the music here will live and people will continue to dance. I believe in "Darlin'" and "Baby." I believe in "Where 'yat?" and "Makin' groceries." I believe in neighborhoods where Mardi Gras Indians sew intricate beaded costumes, kids practice trumpet in the street, and recipes for okra can provide conversation for an entire afternoon.

My family asked me why I wanted to return to New Orleans. "Why do you want to live somewhere where garbage is piled up, rents have doubled, there are no jobs, and houses are filled with black mold? Is it safe? Is it healthy?" They ask if New Orleans is still worth it. I don't have an answer to satisfy them; I can't really even give myself an answer. I keep hearing Louis Armstrong saying, "Man, if ya gotta ask, you'll never know."

I'm just twenty-six, my clothes can all fit in a backpack; I've got a graduate degree in social work and a sixty-five-pound bulldog. I could move anywhere at all, but I believe in this place. I believe I belong here. As hard as it is to live in New Orleans now, it's even harder to imagine living anywhere else.

MIKE MILLER *is a social worker in New Orleans, where he's lived since 1998. He returned to his native Chicago during Hurricane Katrina and then moved back to New Orleans, where only his saxophone was found intact. Miller also tends two local bars and plays third base for a kickball team.*

That Golden Rule Thing

Craig Newmark

I used to share the cynicism common to many nerds—that people were frequently malicious and opportunistic. But of course you don't get treated well wearing a plastic pocket protector and thick black glasses taped together, and now I get that. Years of customer service has changed the way I think about people.

Now I believe that people are overwhelmingly trustworthy and deeply okay. I don't want to sound sanctimonious or syrupy, but for the past seven years I've been doing full-time customer service for Craigslist, interacting with thousands of people. I see that most people share a similar moral compass: They play fair, they give each other a break, and they generally get along. I see that pretty much everyone operates by that Golden Rule thing.

When Katrina hit, for instance, people figured out what other people needed. They didn't ask for permission to re-purpose our New Orleans site. They just turned it into a bulletin board for people to find friends and loved ones. Others offered housing for survivors, and soon jobs were being offered to survivors.

Many of us have lost a sense of neighborhood and com-munity, and we really crave that. In today's culture, some-times we can find that on the Web. Like, it's easy to connect with someone who's just trying to sell a used sofa, and it's really hard to hate a person who's trying to do that.

To be clear, there are bad guys out there and they're drawn to any trust-based, democratic system, like our site. For example, I spend a lot of time dealing with just a few apartment rental brokers in New York who might be, let's say, ethically challenged. A few seem to feel that if others are being sleazy, it's okay for them to do the same. Under pressure from the Craigslist community, though, they are forced to behave. We reason with brokers, explaining our principles, and that usually works.

I started my site to help people help each other. I cre-ated the original platform and then I got out of the way.

The people who run our site really are the people who use it. They are worthy of trust, and I believe in them.

CRAIG NEWMARK *is a customer service representative for Craigslist .org, the online community featuring classified ads and discussion forums he founded in 1995. He is also helping foster Net-based participatory journalism. Newmark lives in San Francisco.*

My Personal Leap of Faith

~

BILL NUNAN

I BELIEVE THAT GOD DOES NOT KNOW the future. I arrived at this belief after a long and difficult journey through—and eventually away from—the faith in which I was raised.

When I was young, many people told me, "God knows everything." For years I tried to force my beliefs to conform to this view. But finally I took my personal leap of faith: I believe that God loves honesty more than conformity. And so I decided to go where the spirit moved me, even if that was away from the spiritual home of my ancestors.

I believe that the fate of our world is not locked in by Scripture, but that the future is shaped by the laws of nature and by what we humans voluntarily do during our time on this planet.

Many people believe every sunrise and sunset, every birth and death, every earthquake, flood, and plague is a voluntary act of God. Like most scientists, I believe that involuntary laws of nature explain the behavior of planets, tectonic plates, weather systems, and viruses. The Earth continually spins and dispassionately quakes. Catastrophes happen infrequently. They are manifestations of the same laws of nature that always govern the universe.

I believe God never tweaks the laws of nature to achieve some desired outcome. Having accepted this, I do not agonize over why God allows evil to occur.

I don't expect God to intervene to help my team win a basketball game, either. As a kid, I thought God knew who would win before the game began. But today I'm convinced nobody knows for sure, not even God.

When I studied science and engineering in college, I met lots of people who had stopped believing in God. They asked, "If science explains the behavior of everything, from electrons to galaxies, then who needs God?"

I decided I still did. I agreed that science eliminates the need for a Creator, but the Creator is only one of the masks of God. The dispassionate mathematical laws of physics seem austere and impersonal, like a star or the moon. But the universe contains more than that. It also includes creatures like us who create purpose and meaning. Gravity does not care, but I do.

Physics does not explain the difference between sound waves and a song, or the difference between sex and love. Physics explains my body, but not my soul.

I believe my soul inspires me to make decisions to diminish pain and increase love in the lives I touch. Lots of times I try, but fail. On a good day I actually get it right! And God is pleasantly surprised.

BILL NUNAN *works as a satellite communications systems engineer. He has electrical engineering degrees from the Massachusetts Institute of Technology and a doctorate in fusion plasma physics from the University of California–Los Angeles. Nunan lives in Manhattan Beach, California, with his wife, Eve Ahlers, and three children.*

Admittance to a Better Life

~

MICHAEL OATMAN

I BELIEVE THAT EDUCATION HAS THE POWER to transform a person's life.

For me, education was the rabbit hole through which I escaped the underclass. I squeezed my three-hundred-pound frame through that hole expecting others to follow and instead I find myself in a strange new land, mostly alone, and wondering at this new life.

For instance, these days for me, dramatic plays at local arts centers have replaced strip pole dancing at the local sleaze huts. I haven't fondled a stripper in years because now I see the stripper through eyes informed by feminist theory.

It's hard to get excited when you're pondering issues of exploitation.

I still wonder what happened to that happy-go-lucky semi-thug that used to hang out with drug dealers on dimly lit street corners. Well, I'm in the library parsing a Jane Austen novel looking for dramatic irony, while many of my old friends are dead or in jail.

I was lucky because I didn't get caught or killed doing something stupid. When I was on the streets, I never felt I was good at anything, but I wrote this poem about a girl who didn't care about me, and it got published. I knew nothing about grammar or syntax, so I went back to school to learn that stuff and one thing led to another.

It's odd to educate oneself away from one's past. As an African-American male I now find myself in a foreign world. Like steam off of a concrete sidewalk I can feel my street cred evaporating away, but I don't fight it anymore. Letting go of the survival tools I needed on the street was a necessary transaction for admittance to a better life.

I am still fighting, but in different ways. I've learned the benefit of research and reading, of debate and listening. My new battlefields are affirmative action, illegal immigration, and institutional racism.

I believe I am the living embodiment of the power of education to change a man. One day soon, a crop of fresh-faced college students will call me professor. I may even be the only black face in the room, the only representative of the underclass. I may feel the slight sting of isolation, but I'll fight it off because I believe in the changes that my education has allowed me to make.

MICHAEL OATMAN *is a playwright, producer, and director living in Cleveland, Ohio. He has been a newspaper reporter and columnist as well as a child care worker with at-risk youth. Oatman is finishing his MFA from Cleveland State University.*

Living What You Do Every Day

∽

Yolanda O'Bannon

I BELIEVE IN BEING WHAT I AM instead of what sounds good to the rest of the world.

Last year, I left a job I hated as a programmer for a job I love as an executive assistant, which is just a fancy word for secretary. I still feel a little embarrassed when people ask me about my new job. Not because of what I do, but because of what some people, including myself, have thought of secretaries.

I had always thought that secretaries were nice and maybe competent but not smart or strong or original. I have a master's degree in English literature, have interviewed the Dalai Lama, and cofounded a nonprofit organization. People who know me wondered why I would go for what seemed to be such a dull and low-status job. Even my new boss asked if I would be bored.

Why would I want to be a secretary? Because it fits me like a glove. I get to do what I love best all day, which is, organize things. I like the challenge of holding the focus on the top priorities in my boss's wildly busy schedule. I can function with a high degree of chaos. Untangling finances feels like playing detective to me. I find filing restful.

The only hard part is dealing with my own and other people's stereotypes, and learning to focus on internal rewards rather than humble appearances. I admit that I feel vaguely embarrassed bringing the faculty lunch or serving coffee to my boss's visitors. But deep down I don't believe that serving food is humiliating. Really, I think of it as a practice in humility. My husband is Tibetan. In Tibetan communities, you serve each other tea as a form of respect. When I'm serving coffee at work, I imagine that I'm serving a monk.

Whenever I get down or defensive about being a secretary, I think of those sharp, fast-talking assistants on *The West Wing*, and how they speak in paragraphs and remember everything, and I feel pretty cool. Sometimes I just look around at my fellow secretaries—savvy and articulate women who are masters at multitasking. I know I'm in good company.

I've done a lot of solo travel in my life—in New Zealand, Japan, Africa, and India. Taking this job was harder than any of that. When I said I was going to spend a year in northern India, I'd get points. When I said I was going to be a secretary, people wondered what happened to me.

It would be easier if I were someone whose skills were more respected and better compensated—a doctor, an architect, a scientist. I would feel cool when I meet someone at a party. But a friend reminded me that you only have to talk about what you do for five minutes at parties, but you have to live what you do every day of your life, so better to do what you love, and forget about how it looks. And this, I believe.

YOLANDA O'BANNON *is executive assistant to biochemist and former National Academy of Sciences president Bruce Alberts. O'Bannon was born in Phoenix and was raised on air force bases around the world. She lives with her husband in Richmond, California.*

The Long Road to Forgiveness

~

KIM PHUC

ON JUNE 8, 1972, I RAN out from Cao Dai temple in my village, Trang Bang, South Vietnam, I saw an airplane getting lower and then four bombs falling down. I saw fire everywhere around me. Then I saw the fire over my body, especially on my left arm. My clothes had been burned off by fire.

I was nine years old but I still remember my thoughts at that moment: I would be ugly and people would treat me in a different way. My picture was taken in that moment on Road 1 from Saigon to Phnom Penh. After a soldier gave me some drink and poured water over my body, I lost my consciousness.

Several days after, I realized that I was in the hospital, where I spent fourteen months and had seventeen operations. It was a very difficult time for me when I went home from the hospital. Our house was destroyed, we lost everything, and we just survived day-by-day.

Although I suffered from pain, itching, and headaches all the time, the long hospital stay made me dream to become a doctor. But my studies were cut short by the local government. They wanted me as a symbol of the state. I could not go to school anymore.

The anger inside me was like a hatred as high as a mountain. I hated my life. I hated all people who were normal because I was not normal. I really wanted to die many times.

I spent my daytime in the library to read a lot of religious books to find a purpose for my life. One of the books that I read was the Holy Bible. On Christmas 1982, I accepted Jesus Christ as my personal Savior. It was an amazing turning point in my life. God helped me to learn to forgive—the most difficult of all lessons. It didn't happen in a day and it wasn't easy. But I finally got it.

Forgiveness made me free from hatred. I still have many scars on my body and severe pain most days, but my heart is cleansed.

Napalm is very powerful, but faith, forgiveness, and

love are much more powerful. We would not have war at all if everyone could learn how to live with true love, hope, and forgiveness. If that little girl in the picture can do it, ask yourself: Can you?

KIM PHUC *is best known as "the girl in the picture," the provocative photo of a Vietnam War napalm attack. Phuc was nine years old when she was pictured running naked and screaming on a road near Saigon, her skin burning from the explosions. She now lives in Canada and works to aid children who are war victims. (This essay was produced by Anne Penman for the Canadian Broadcasting Corporation.)*

The Practice of Slowing Down

PHIL POWERS

I BELIEVE IN THE IMPORTANCE OF PACE. I grew up in a frenetic household, both parents working jobs that demanded their attention 24/7. I was little and fast and rushed around, and I still have that person inside me, always at risk of moving too quickly, missing the connection, making mistakes.

The forest behind our house offered a peaceful respite. My passion for the vertical world took me from tall trees in my backyard to climbing steep cliffs and crags. As a teen, I was moving easily over the landscapes of the American West and was drawn to higher summits. When I was nineteen, I learned something called the "rest step" from an old mountain climber named Paul Petzoldt. He advised me to rest in the middle of each step completely, but briefly. The rest step, which I still practice today, allows me to walk or climb with little effort. I can move very quickly yet still find a pause in every step.

The awareness of pace I owe to my teacher has served me whether I am seeking the world's highest summits, sharing my love for the mountains with others, or kneeling to look my son, Gus, in the eye when he has a question.

It serves me as I drive, adjusting my speed to gain a bit of calm and reach my destination only minutes behind the "record time" a faster lane might provide. It serves me at home where we maintain a tradition of gathering each night at the dinner table to eat and talk to each other.

In times of crisis, pace comes to my aid. Another of Petzoldt's lessons was when faced with an emergency, sit down, collect yourself, make a plan. When needs seem most urgent—even life-threatening—the practice of slowing down offers calm and clarity.

In 1987, I was in Pakistan to climb Gasherbrum II, one of the world's highest peaks. We were a small group and it was a very big mountain. Our expedition faced more than its share of difficulty: A long storm wiped out most of our food rations and an avalanche devastated our camp, obliterating our tents. One of our party developed altitude sickness; blood poisoning threatened another. In the face of each disaster, we carefully developed a new plan. Snow caves replaced lost tents. Soups replaced full meals. Eventually we climbed slowly to the top, then made our way safely down.

Concentrating on how I move through the world is important. It's why I reach mountain summits and life goals with energy to spare.

There is magic in any faith. Every once in a while, rushing about, my belief in pace rises up, slows me down, and grants me a view of a sunset, a smile from a stranger, or a conversation with a child. I owe these moments to what I learned from an old mountain climber and have practiced ever since.

PHIL POWERS *is the executive director of the American Alpine Club. He has made dozens of mountaineering expeditions to Alaska, Asia, and South America since he began climbing as a boy in Oklahoma. Powers has written two books on mountain-climbing and lives in Denver with his wife and children.*

Living My Prayer

~

SISTER HELEN PREJEAN

I WATCH WHAT I DO TO SEE what I really believe.

Belief and faith are not just words. It's one thing for me to say I'm a Christian, but I have to embody what it means; I have to live it. So, writing this essay and knowing I'll share it in a public way becomes an occasion for me to look deeply at what I really believe by how I act.

"Love your neighbor as yourself," Jesus said, and as a beginner nun I tried earnestly to love my neighbor—the children I taught, their parents, my fellow teachers, my fellow nuns. But for a long time the circle of my loving care was small and, for the most part, included only white, middle-class people like me. But one day I woke up to Jesus's deeper challenge to love the outcast, the criminal, the underdog. So I packed my stuff and moved into a noisy, violent housing project in an African-American neighborhood in New Orleans.

I saw the suffering and I let myself feel it: the sound of gunshots in the night, mothers calling out for their children. I saw the injustice and was compelled to do something about it. I changed from being a nun who only prayed for the suffering world to a nun with my sleeves rolled up, living my prayer. Working in that community in New Orleans soon led me to Louisiana's death row.

So I keep watching what I do to see what I actually believe.

Jesus's biggest challenge to us is to love our enemies. On death row I encountered the enemy, those considered so irredeemable by our society that even our Supreme Court has made it legal to kill them. For twenty years now I've been visiting people on death row, and I have accompanied six human beings to their deaths. As each has been killed I have told them to look at me. I want them to see a loving face when they die. I want my face to carry the love that tells them that they and every one of us are worth more than our most terrible acts.

But I knew being with the perpetrators wasn't enough. I

also had to reach out to victims' families. I visited the families who wanted to see me, and I founded a victims' support group in New Orleans. It was a big stretch for me, loving both perpetrators and victims' families, and most of the time I fail because so often the victims' families interpret my care for perpetrators as choosing sides—the wrong side. I understand that, but I don't stop reaching out.

I've learned from victims' families just how alone many of them feel. The murder of their loved one is so horrible, their pain so great, that most people stay away. But they need people to visit, to listen, to care. It doesn't take anybody special, just someone who cares.

Writing this essay reminds me, as an ordinary person, that it's important to take stock, to see where I am. The only way I know what I really believe is by keeping watch over what I do.

SISTER HELEN PREJEAN's *work as spiritual adviser to death row inmates formed the basis of two books, including* Dead Man Walking. *A native of Louisiana, Prejean became a nun in 1957, and in 1981 she dedicated her life to the poor of New Orleans.*

The Chance to Move Forward

Maria Mayo Robbins

I BELIEVE IN CHANCE.

Strings of unexpected encounters mark my life. I believe that chance has guided me—jolted me sometimes—onto paths I wouldn't have chosen but needed to follow whether I knew it or not. Chance encounters have led me across continents and into unanticipated worlds.

At twenty-one, I first visited Italy. As I struggled with a mouthful of college Italian to find the word for "towel" in a hostel one morning, an older woman laughed, straightened out my garbled attempts, and invited me to her home. Chance gently pushed me, and led me to a lifelong connection to her family, their small town of Castelfranco Veneto, and, several years later, the opportunity to live there.

But chance is not always kind. When I was twenty-five years old, chance led an intruder to break into my home in the middle of a quiet spring night. The violence of that night and months of rehabilitation left me questioning how I could ever find meaning in such a vicious stroke of fortune. But in the years that followed I drew even closer to my family and became a more empathetic friend. I relished the ability to walk, or even run, on my own. I did all the things I had always wanted to do: I pierced my nose, flew to Israel, and hauled a rented grand piano up to my eighth-floor apartment. I lived a life in vivid moments. I followed the questions raised by the attack into graduate school, where today I continue to study and work for justice for victims of violence. I kept going, and meaning took hold in unexpected places.

As a student of religion, I read and write about people and texts that desperately seek cosmic order in a world of chaos. Coincidence threatens the divine order of creation and must be explained. For myself, I believe that chance creates order in the world. We can't choreograph life events, but we can clasp the hands of those who appear in our paths and see where they lead us. So many chance encounters have moved me forward, offering me direction and a sense of purpose, if I was willing to follow.

My belief in chance lets me see life as brimming with possibility: the person next to me in line at the airport who becomes a lifelong friend, the professor in the elevator who asks a provocative question, or the soldier I meet at an outdoor café in Jerusalem who takes me on a romantic tour of the city, leaving me with an indelible memory.

And as much as I have resisted saying this for many years, even the unwelcome and cruel strikes of chance must somehow find their place in the order of our lives. Believing this—believing in chance—I can always pick up my body and move forward.

MARIA MAYO ROBBINS *is a doctoral candidate in religion at Vanderbilt University in Nashville, Tennessee. She also teaches biblical languages at a local college and is writing a book about forgiveness.*

Utterly Humbled by Mystery

～

Father Richard Rohr

I BELIEVE IN MYSTERY AND MULTIPLICITY. To religious believers this may sound almost pagan. But I don't think so. My very belief and experience of a loving and endlessly creative God has led me to trust in both.

I've had the good fortune of teaching and preaching across much of the globe, while also struggling to make sense of my experience in my own tiny world. This life journey has led me to love mystery, and not feel the need to change it or make it un-mysterious. This has put me at odds with many other believers I know who seem to need explanations for everything.

Religious belief has made me comfortable with ambiguity. "Hints and guesses," as T. S. Eliot would say. I often spend the season of Lent in a hermitage, where I live alone for the whole forty days. The more I am alone with the Alone, the more I surrender to ambivalence, to happy contradictions and seeming inconsistencies in myself and almost everything else, including God. Paradoxes don't scare me anymore.

When I was young, I couldn't tolerate such ambiguity. My education had trained me to have a lust for answers and explanations. Now at age sixty-three, it's all quite different. I no longer believe this is a quid pro quo universe—I've counseled too many prisoners, worked with too many failed marriages, faced my own dilemmas too many times, and been loved gratuitously after too many failures.

Whenever I think there's a perfect pattern, further reading and study reveal an exception. Whenever I want to say "only" or "always," someone or something proves me wrong. My scientist friends have come up with things like "principles of uncertainty" and dark holes. They're willing to live inside imagined hypotheses and theories. But many religious folks insist on *answers* that are *always* true. We love closure, resolution, and clarity, while thinking that we are people of "faith"! How strange that the very word "faith" has come to mean its exact opposite.

People who have really met the Holy are always humble. It's the people who don't know who usually pretend that they do. People who've had any genuine spiritual experience always know that they *don't know*. They are utterly humbled before mystery. They are in awe before the abyss of it all, in wonder at eternity and depth, and a Love, which is incomprehensible to the mind. It is a litmus test for authentic God experience, and is—quite sadly—absent from much of our religious conversation today. My belief and comfort are in the depths of Mystery, which should be the very task of religion.

RICHARD ROHR *is founder of the Center for Action and Contemplation in Albuquerque, New Mexico. He took his Franciscan vows in 1961 and was ordained as a priest in 1970. Rohr is a frequent speaker and writer on issues of community building, peace, and justice.*

I Always Have a Choice

CATHERINE ROYCE

I BELIEVE THAT I ALWAYS HAVE A choice. No matter what I'm doing. No matter where I am. No matter what is happening to me. I always have a choice.

Today I am sitting at my computer, speaking these words through a microphone. Although I have spent my life typing on a keyboard, I can no longer use my hands. Every day I sit at my computer speaking words instead of typing. In 2003, I was diagnosed with ALS, Lou Gehrig's disease. Over time, this disease will weaken and finally destroy every significant muscle in my body. Ultimately, I will be unable to move, to speak, and finally, to breathe. Already, I am largely dependent upon others. So every day I review my choices.

Living with ALS seems a bit like going into the witness protection program. Everything I have ever known about myself, how I look, how I act, how I interact with the world, is rapidly and radically changing. And yet, with each change, I still have choice. When I could no longer type with my hands, I knew I could give up writing entirely or go through the arduous process of learning how to use voice recognition software. I'm not a young woman. This took real work. Interestingly, I write more now than ever before.

And at an even more practical level, every day I choose not only how I will live, but if I will live. I have no particular religious mandate that forbids contemplating a shorter life, an action that would deny this disease its ultimate expression. But this is where my belief in choice truly finds its power. I can choose to see ALS as nothing more than a death sentence or I can choose to see it as an invitation—an opportunity to learn who I truly am.

Even people in the witness protection program must take with them fundamental aspects of themselves which can never change. What are these aspects for me? This is what I learn every day, and so far I have discovered many unique things, but one stands out above the rest. I have discovered in myself an ability to recognize, give, and receive caring in a way far deeper than anything in my life previously. Others have seen this in me as well.

I, who have always been an intensely private and independent person, have allowed a wide circle of family and friends into the most intimate parts of my life. Previously, I would have found such a prospect appalling. I might have felt I had no choice but to embrace the assumption that living with ALS means a life of hardship and isolation. Instead, because I believe that I always have a choice, I opened myself to other possibilities. And now the very thing that at first seemed so abhorrent has graced my life with unaccustomed sweetness. It was always there. Only now I have chosen to see it. This sweetness underscores and celebrates my belief that I always have a choice.

CATHERINE ROYCE *was diagnosed with ALS when she was fifty-five. She was a dancer for thirty years and a former deputy art commissioner for the city of Boston. Royce lives in Dorchester, Massachusetts, where she writes every day, using her microphone and voice recognition software.*

I Am Not My Body

~

Lisa Sandin

I believe I am not my body.

Every day, we see images of perfect bodies we can never have, and we become convinced our bodies are who we are. Passing through puberty, into adulthood, and now into middle age, I've wasted a lot of time lamenting the size of my hips, the gray in my hair, and the lines in my face. Finally, as I approach my fifties, I believe my parents were right all along: I am not my body.

I was born in 1959, at the tail end of the baby boom. Unfortunately I arrived without all my body parts fully intact. My left arm is a short stub with a small hand and three fingers, reminiscent of a thalidomide defect. To my good fortune, I had superb parents. They were fighters who struck "I can't" from my vocabulary and replaced it with "I will find a way." They believed the development of the mind, heart, and soul determines who you are and who you will become. My body was not to be used as an excuse; instead it was a catalyst.

My body was not neglected, though. It endured surgery; it was dragged to physical therapy, then to swimming, and finally to yoga. But it was not the focus of my life. I was taught to respect my body, but to remember that it was only a vehicle that carried the important things: my brain and soul. Moreover, I was taught that bodies come in all shapes, colors, and sizes, and that everyone was struggling in some way with their physical inadequacies. Infomercials have convinced me this must be true, although through adolescence I found it difficult to believe the cheerleading squad had any self-doubts.

In my alternately formed body, I have learned lessons about patience, determination, frustration, and success. This body can't play the piano or climb rock walls, but it taught all the neighborhood kids to eat with their feet, a skill it learned in the children's hospital. Eventually it learned to tie shoes, crossed a stage to pick up a college diploma, backpacked through Europe, and changed my baby's diapers.

Some people think I am my body and treat me with prejudice or pity. Some are just curious. It took years, but I have learned to ignore the stares and just smile back. My body has taught me to respect my fellow humans—even the thin, able-bodied, beautiful ones.

I am my words, my ideas, and my actions. I am filled with love, humor, ambition, and intelligence. This I believe: I am your fellow human being and, like you, I am so much more than a body.

LISA SANDIN *lives with her husband, Pasquale Di Raddo, and two teenage children in Big Rapids, Michigan. She teaches yoga and meditation classes and helps her autistic son with his schoolwork. Sandin's essay was first published in* USA Weekend *magazine.*

Resilience Is a Gift

〜

Joel Schmidt

I LISTEN TO PEOPLE FOR A LIVING. As a psychologist in the Department of Veterans Affairs, I hear about some of the worst experiences humans have to bear. I have sat face-to-face with a Bataan Death March survivor, an airman shot down over Germany, a Marine who was at the Chosin Reservoir, veterans from every region of Vietnam, medics and infantry soldiers from Afghanistan and Iraq. I have spoken with people who have been assaulted and brutalized by their own comrades—and parents who've had to attend their own children's funerals.

I have gained a surprising belief from hearing about so

much agony: I believe in the power of human resilience. I am continually inspired by the ability of the emotionally wounded to pick themselves up and keep going after enduring the most traumatic circumstances imaginable.

Iraq veterans describe to me the constant hell of unpredictable IED attacks and invisible snipers. By the time they get home, many can't drive on the freeway or be in the same room with old friends. One vet described being locked in an emotional cage between numbness and rage.

Emerging from this terrible backdrop, many Iraq vets have surprised me with their drive to recover and their unpredictable ways of giving back some meaning to their lives. For example, there was a veteran whose most powerful therapeutic experience was helping his grandmother keep her small business running. This cause gave him a reason to care, someone to emotionally connect with, and ultimately a reason to get up in the morning.

This might sound like naive optimism when in fact treatment is often long and hard, and not every story has a happy ending. Some days when I go home my head hurts. I feel sad or worried or angry or ineffective. On these days, I have to appeal to my own strategies for self-care, pick myself back up, and keep going.

I went to school to learn how to help people get better. Instead, it is often the very people I have spent my career trying to help who remind me how to care for myself. I keep a catalog of them in my head, and I try to use this list as a road map, an inspiration, and a reminder of what human resilience can achieve.

I make it a point to compliment the strength and ingenuity of the people who sit in my office. But the truth is, I don't think many of them realize the depth of my admiration. Sitting in the room with these people every day allows me to hope that I might also find strength to face future problems. This solid sense of hope is a gift, and it is my humble desire to share it with the next person who sits with me.

JOEL SCHMIDT *is a clinical psychologist at the Veterans Affairs Mental Health Clinic in Oakland, California. He is also training director for a psychology internship program in the VA health care system. Schmidt lives with his wife near San Francisco Bay.*

The Designated Celebrator

MELINDA SHOAF

I BELIEVE THAT IF YOU'RE THE PERSON in your family who arranged for and executed the celebration this past holiday season, well, you're probably still tired. You may be wondering why you spent so much on presents, why you had to have your house just right, why you had friends over for drinks when you were already weary and worn out. You may be thinking that you're getting too old for all of this or you may be thinking you're too young.

If you know what I'm talking about, you're probably your family's Designated Celebrator—that is, the one who sees to it that a holiday actually happens in the lives of your loved ones.

After New Year's, I was sitting at the breakfast table in a stupor. My husband asked if I was all right.

"I'm exhausted," I answered. "I'm totally exhausted."

He looked puzzled. "Why do you do this to yourself every year?"

I have to admit that part of what I do around the winter holidays seems almost involuntary, innate. It's as if I'm driven by the ancient need to mark the darkness of winter with my little bit of light.

My answer to my husband's question is that I believe one of the most important things I can do while I'm on this planet is honor those I love through celebrations, and the older I get, the more I believe it.

When my children were small, their father lost his job. It took a decade to recover emotionally and financially. Hot water and electricity were luxuries that weren't always available; meals were a challenge. I tried to hide it from them, but I was constantly afraid of losing our home. Those celebrations were so sparse, the future so uncertain, that the ground seemed to be shifting beneath us.

So now, celebrations mean that much more to me. This year, I polished the silver, lit the candles, made sure a sprig of holly was carefully tacked above every window; I served a $12 bottle of wine instead of a $7 one; I bought lamb chops instead of a roast—little things, just so we'd remember this day, this night.

I believe that in this world there is and always has been so much sadness and sorrow, so much uncertainty, that if we didn't set aside time for merriment, gifts, music, and laughter with family and friends, we might just forget to celebrate altogether. We'd just plod along in life.

I believe in the importance of celebrations. As my family's Designated Celebrator I may be tired and I may not have done all that I set out to do, but I believe that this year, I celebrated the ones I love, and I hope with all my heart that I celebrated them well.

Writer and homemaker MELINDA SHOAF *marks the holidays with her four grown children in Memphis, Tennessee, where she lives with her husband and two dogs. She says her oldest daughter will likely carry on the Designated Celebrator tradition in the family.*

Baking by Senses and Memories

~

EMILY SMITH

I HAVE GONE THROUGH TEN POUNDS OF flour in three months.
I know that's not normal, but I believe baking is an expression of love—not only for the person being baked for, but
also for the person who taught me how to bake, for the person who gave me the recipe, for the past and tradition.

Grandma Dottie lives on in her recipes that I continue
to bake. Her molasses cookies are so good they need to be
shared with the world. The batter is sticky and has to be re-
frigerated for four hours. It turns the whole thing into more
of a production, but it's impossible to roll the dough into
balls when it's that sticky. I know; I've tried.

So I wait—just like my grandmother waited—four hours, while the dough chills. Then I roll the dough into balls, roll the dough balls in sugar and smash them with a fork twice, creating a crisscross pattern, and put them in the oven. I look at the cookies instead of relying on the timer. I'm beginning to bake with my senses and my memory instead of with the recipe.

My grandma Dottie abbreviated everything in her recipes so it took me a while to figure it out. Is the batter the right color, the right consistency, does it smell right? My dad's job is to compare my reproductions to the originals of his childhood. If they turn out the same, they're more than cookies— and that's what I'm trying to do. I like to watch my father's face when he remembers his mother.

Because we're Texan, my mother needs a pecan pie for it to really be Thanksgiving. Pecan pie is mostly corn syrup, a few eggs, and pecans. It doesn't look appetizing. But amazing things happen in the oven. The filling caramelizes and turns a dark brown. I baked my mom a pecan pie. I made the crust and everything—and even she doesn't do that. The recipe I used yields a stiffer filling. It's not the gooey pecan pie I grew up with. So I was worried at first that I'd done something wrong. But my mother said it was the best pecan pie she'd ever had.

And right then and there *my* pecan pie recipe, the one

that I'd found in the cookbook my grandmother gave me, became the new family recipe. So, this Thanksgiving it's my job to make the pie. For me, it's a symbol of becoming an adult, and the pecan pie becomes my contribution to our family tradition.

I believe that as long as I keep baking, my grandmother hasn't really gone. I believe baking is the best way for me to express love for my people in the present, and honor the people of my past, all in one batch.

EMILY SMITH *majored in English and Spanish literature at the University of Texas in her hometown of Austin. Smith plans to become a minister in the United Methodist Church after finishing a master of divinity degree at Atlanta's Emory University.*

Learning to Trust My Intuition

CYNTHIA SOMMER

I BELIEVE IN INTUITION—THAT FEELING YOU have about something or someone, without knowing quite why. Intuition is defined as "knowing or sensing without the use of rational processes." I'm not sure if that's a fair assessment; it suggests that intuition is irrational.

As a Latina, I come from a culture that acknowledges the supernatural and is rooted in indigenous traditions aligned closely with nature. I grew up with a grandmother who administered herbal home remedies and applied concoctions like olive oil and salt to bumps on the head. She also listened as we retold our dreams, helping to decipher their meanings. The passing of a loved one was always less surprising after dreaming of doves.

I'm only recently learning to trust my intuition again. Over a decade ago, I purposefully made the investment in an MBA to develop my analytical skills. By graduation, I had learned the process of being rational. My first job post-MBA was as an analyst. As my career progressed, so did the analytics. I began to believe less in my intuition. Budgets, metrics, research, and ratios: My form of expression became much more calculated.

All of which served me well until I became executive director of a cultural arts center promoting Chicano, Latino, and indigenous culture. Every day I was with artists who wholly embraced intuition as a driving force for their creativity—and *cultura* as a way to express it, be it through Danza Azteca Flor y Canto, or *teatro*.

About the same time, I found myself drawn to anything with the shape or image of a lizard. When buying inventory for the *centro*, I always selected products with lizards—and they sold well. I figured I was simply making good retail choices, but a community elder suggested the lizard may be my totem. She told me the lizard is associated with the dream life, and that individuals with a lizard totem should listen to their own intuition over anyone else's. A lizard's tail will detach from the body, literally leaving behind a part of itself in order to survive. The elder suggested that what I needed to lose was my "corporate"-ness.

It seems I had come full circle.

The lizard brought me back around to counting on my intuition as much as the numbers. And just as I listened to my grandmother and mother conversing about their dreams and intuition, so do my children. They know that what they're feeling can be trusted in making decisions and judgments. And they're comfortable sharing their dreams with us. So I believe in intuition. For me, it feels like the right thing to do.

CYNTHIA SOMMER *lives in Folsom, California. She is vice president of marketing for PRIDE Industries, a nonprofit employer of people with disabilities. Sommer is active in community service and teaches business and marketing courses at local colleges.*

An Optimistic View of the World

DAN TANI

LIKE MANY PEOPLE, I HAVE A JOB that requires me to take a business trip every now and then. I'm on one right now. As I write this, I'm flying over New Zealand; it looks so beautiful out the window. Unlike most people, however, I'm traveling over 200 miles above the Earth, and I'm going 17,500 miles an hour.

When I look down, I am stunned by the intense colors of the Earth, the intricate patterns and textures, and sheer beauty of our home planet. When I watch the Earth roll by, I realize I believe in optimism.

It would be hard to believe that there is no hope for

Earth from up here. The International Space Station is a collaboration of sixteen nations—and one of our primary partners was our sworn enemy only a few decades ago. The space station itself is the embodiment of where we can go as a global society.

My own optimism is rooted in two very different ideas: statistical probability and trust.

First, I accept the statistical probability that I am not likely to be killed by a terrorist or contract some horrible disease. It's not that I think that everything will work out okay; it's that I think that everything will *probably* work out okay.

And second, trust. I learned trust from my mother, and in a way this essay is for her. Two months ago, while I was up here, she died in an accident, and of course I have been unable to return to honor her. I have been thinking about her life, which was not an easy one. She was born into poverty, forcibly relocated during World War II, survived the premature deaths of her husband and a son—and yet, her outlook was so life-affirming. She felt that people were good and well-meaning. Sometimes I felt that she trusted too easily, and I was afraid that that stranger she talked to on the street or the airplane might not be as nice as she thought. But I was almost always proven wrong, and I'm so grateful for her example.

I came to believe, like her, that most people want to live their lives without conflict. They care about the other people in their house, their neighborhood, their country, and their planet.

I am an astronaut, and I cannot imagine doing what I'm doing, seeing what I'm seeing, and not being an optimist. We climb aboard extremely complex machines which hurl us into space, and we have to trust that every engineer, every technician, and every manager has done their job, and that we have a high statistical probability of success.

And once we are here, we get to look back and see the Earth as a thing of stunning beauty. Of course, I know there are awful things going on down there, that people are in pain, wars are raging, poverty and hunger are taking far too many lives—but from here, I can only see the whole.

I wish that everyone could see the world from my perspective; I believe that more people would be optimistic about our future.

DAN TANI *served as flight engineer on the International Space Station where he conducted four space walks. He joined the National Aeronautics and Space Administration as an astronaut candidate in 1996. Tani was raised in Lombard, Illinois, by his mother, and now lives with his wife and children in Houston.*

Community in Action

Studs Terkel

My own beliefs, my personal beliefs, came into being during the most traumatic moment in American history: the Great American Depression of the 1930s. I was seventeen at the time, and I saw on the sidewalks pots and pans and bedsteads and mattresses. A family had just been evicted and there was an individual cry of despair, multiplied by millions. But that community had a number of people on that very block who were electricians and plumbers and carpenters and they appeared that same evening, the evening of the eviction, and moved these household goods back into the flat where they had been. They turned on the gas; they fixed the plumbing. It was a community in action accomplishing something.

And this is my belief, too: that it's the community in action that accomplishes more than any individual does, no matter how strong he may be.

Einstein once observed that Westerners have a feeling the individual loses his freedom if he joins, say, a union or any group. Precisely the opposite's the case. The individual discovers his strength as an individual because he has, along the way, discovered others share his feelings—he is not alone, and thus a community is formed. You might call it the prescient community or the prophetic community. It's always been there.

And I must say, it has always paid its dues, too. The community of the '30s and '40s and the Depression, fighting for rights of laborers and the rights of women and the rights of all people who are different from the majority, always paid their dues. But it was their presence as well as their prescience that made for whatever progress we have made.

And that's what Tom Paine meant when he said: "Freedom has been hunted around the globe; reason was considered as rebellion; and the slavery of fear made men afraid to think. But such is the irresistible nature of truth that all it asks, all it wants, is the liberty of appearing. In such a situation, man becomes what he ought to be."

Still quoting Tom Paine: "He sees his species not with the inhuman idea of a natural enemy"—you're either with us or against us, no. "He sees his species as kindred."

And that happens to be my belief, and I'll put it into three words: community in action.

Born in 1912, Pulitzer Prize–winning oral historian STUDS TERKEL moved to Chicago shortly before the Great Depression. Although trained as a lawyer, he worked as an actor, sportscaster, deejay, writer, and interviewer. Terkel hosted a Chicago radio program for forty-five years and has authored twelve oral histories about twentieth-century America.

Music Makes Me Come Alive

Joan Tower

After sixty-plus years of composing and performing, I believe more than ever in the extraordinary power of music.

In this day of fast information and communication, music nourishes our inner souls. As tensions between nations continue, music reaches beyond borders. At weddings, funerals, inaugurations, and parades, music gives us public permission to feel and share things. In fact, music has always been a shared thing—between the creator, the performer, and the audience. Music connects me to people I don't even know.

Strong music puts you in a space where you forget

about yourself. It's like a good movie. It's an escape. You lose yourself. It's a license to feel, sing, shout, and to dance.

Do you remember when you first fell in love? Was there a song associated with that love? When you hear that song now, do you think of that person and actually remember what you felt? Maybe you even cry.

When I was growing up, my life largely centered around boys and sex. I was into music, but music didn't always give me the nourishment that boys did. It takes time and patience to be nourished by music. Now, I can say, without music I would be lost.

A conductor once told me that music had kept him off the streets and even out of jail. Music became a kind of "survival" phenomenon for him (and for me, too). It is our drug of choice because it has given us the extraordinary lasting inner experience that has even replaced real drugs, vacations, money, fame, and all the things we associate with pleasure and excitement. A friend of mine who happens to be an extraordinary pianist and still practices up to five hours a day once said to me, "The piano is my best friend. I can't think of anyone better to spend my time with."

I feel the same way about composing. I'm in the studio from 1:00 to 5:30 religiously, every day. I used to run from the studio—I'd tell myself I had to clean or make a telephone call, anything to get out of there. Now I look forward to these hours. Composing is slow—I wait for the right notes. The hardest thing is to get your soul down on the page and have it come out on the other side in a way that works.

Music is not just my most trusted friend. It makes me come alive, to show strength and passion and to feel useful. Music makes me feel like I'm doing something terribly important. I believe that with music I can help to change the world around me—if just a little bit.

Composer and pianist JOAN TOWER was born in New York and spent her youth in Bolivia where her father worked as a mining engineer. Her most famous works include "Fanfares for the Uncommon Woman" and the tone poem "Sequoia." Tower teaches at Bard College.

God Is God Because He Remembers

ELIE WIESEL

I REMEMBER MAY 1944. I WAS FIFTEEN and a half. And I was thrown into a haunted universe where the story of the human adventure seemed to swing irrevocably between horror and malediction. I remember, I remember because I was there with my father. I was still living with him there. We worked together. We returned to the camp together. We stayed in the same block. We slept in the same box. We shared bread and soup. Never were we so close to one another. We talked a lot to each other, especially in the evenings, but never of death. I believed, I hoped that I would not survive him. Not even for one day. Without saying it to him, I thought I was the last of our line. With him, our past would die. With me, our future.

The moment the war ended, I believed—we all did—that anyone who survived death must bear witness. Some of us even believed that they survived in order to become witnesses. But then I knew deep down that it would be impossible to communicate the entire story. Nobody can. I personally decided to wait, to see, during ten years, if I would be capable to find the proper words, the proper pace, the proper melody, or maybe even the proper silence to describe the ineffable.

For in my tradition, as a Jew, I believe that whatever we receive we must share. When we endure an experience, the experience cannot stay with me alone. It must be opened. It must become an offering. It must be deepened and given and shared. And of course I am afraid that memories suppressed could come back with a fury, which is dangerous to all human beings, not only to those who directly were participants but to people everywhere, to the world, for everyone. And so, therefore, those memories that are discarded, shamed, somehow they may come back in different ways, disguised. Perhaps seeking another outlet.

Granted, our task is to inform. But information must be transformed into knowledge, knowledge into sensitivity, and sensitivity into commitment.

How can we therefore speak, unless we believe that our words have meaning, that our words will help others to prevent my past from becoming another person's—another people's—future. Yes, our stories are essential. Essential to memory. I believe that the witnesses, especially the survivors, have the most important role. They can simply say, in the words of the prophet, I was there. What is a witness if not someone who has a tale to tell and lives only with one haunting desire—to tell it. Without memory, there is no culture. Without memory, there would be no civilization. No society. No future.

After all God is God because He remembers.

Writer, political activist, and Holocaust survivor ELIE WIESEL *is the author of more than forty books concerning Judaism, the Holocaust, and the moral responsibility of all people to fight intolerance, racism, and injustice. Wiesel was awarded the Nobel Peace Prize in 1986.*

The Guts to Keep Going

AMY LYLES WILSON

I BELIEVE IN OLD WOMEN WHO LEARN new tricks—gutsy, wrinkled broads who eat alone in restaurants and pump their own gas.

When my father died six years ago, my mother, then seventy-nine, had already done quite a lot. She had moved from her hometown in Mississippi to work in the big city even though many of her generation stayed put. She had raised three daughters, chaired PTAs, volunteered for a host of causes, and nursed her husband through heart surgery. Along the way, she lost a breast and part of her colon to cancer.

What she had not done before Daddy's death, however, was pump her own gas. After the funeral, when she stopped the car at the filling station, neither of us moved. We were both waiting, I guess, for Daddy to wink at us before sliding out to "fill 'er up."

As I collected myself and turned to open the door, my mother said, "I guess you better show me how this works."

After we finished she asked, "That's it?" "Yes ma'am," I said, "you'll do fine." I tried not to think of all the things my mother would now have to do by herself.

As we drove off, Mother told me about her old friend Betty Ann whose husband, Carl, had died recently. It seems Betty Ann got in the passenger seat of their new Buick and waited a full three minutes for Carl to appear behind the wheel before finally hauling herself to the other side of the car and driving downtown. Telling me this story, my mother was crying just a bit. She said, "I guess you do what you have to do."

I did not marry until age forty-one, so I know about pumping gas and eating alone in restaurants. But I haven't a clue what it's like to lose your soul mate unexpectedly after fifty-two years of marriage, leaving you to deal not only with grief but also with car mechanics. Mother has always been a quick study, though, so it was not long before she could tell her widowed friends which Exxon had the lowest prices, which BP still offered full service, which Chevron was well-lighted at dusk.

There have been other challenges for my mother, of course, since my father died. From downsizing the family home to allowing a widower preacher to "go Dutch" with her at the Olive Garden on occasion, my mother has put one foot in front of the other with grace and fortitude.

It is a small thing, perhaps, to believe in elderly women doing nothing more than putting gas into cars and getting themselves from point A to point B without an escort. But to my mind, and heart, it's a belief in something much bigger than that: the guts to keep going.

AMY LYLES WILSON *is a writer and editor in Nashville, Tennessee. She is studying theology at Vanderbilt University Divinity School and is working on a book about grief.*

Freeing Myself Through Forgiveness

Yolanda Young

RECENTLY I E-MAILED MY FATHER. I WROTE: "It was good to hear from you. I'm glad you're well. Take care." I last heard from him when he e-mailed my Web page wishing me a happy belated birthday. He wrote in February. My birthday was in October.

Forgetting my birthday is the least of my father's failings. I was five when my parents divorced. He moved across the country and I rarely saw or heard from him. When I was seventeen, I watched him beat a woman in the street. His violence wasn't a revelation. I'd already witnessed him shoot my mother.

Here's where you gasp, look upon me with pitying eyes, and assume that I must hate my father. I don't. His last act of violence against my mother was in some ways a lucky break. My mother went right on living, and through her I came to believe in the power of forgiveness.

She never complained about his not paying child support. On the rare occasions that he called or visited, the woman insisted that I be respectful. Momma always made the distinction: My father hurt her, not me. Sure there were moments when he pissed me off—when he blamed my mother for the shooting or berated me for asking for money while I was in college. Five years later he was offended when I didn't invite him to my law school graduation. Despite all this, he is still my father. When he is sick, I call and check on him. When he dies, if there is no money, a likelihood, I will bury him.

While I'm not fond of my father, I may be the only family member who does not despise him. I believe this is because I never loved him. When I was a child, I was open to it, but he wasn't around and hard to love when he was. But I didn't miss not having a father thanks to the daily presence of my grandfather and uncles. They taught me to play basketball and spades, and arranged modest vacations to Six Flags and the Bayou Classic. Some say having my father do these things would have been better, in much the same way that not growing up poor would have been better, but I believe what has made the difference is that I grew up happy and loved.

There are ways in which I'm very much my father's daughter. My height, eyes, and premature graying are thanks to him. I have his stubborn streak and, on rare occasions, his temper; but I also possess his ambition and ingenuity.

A few years after law school when I declined to handle a legal matter for him, he told me that he was cutting me off. "If that's what you want," I replied, understanding my father's emotional struggles but not becoming hostage to them. Now he is appealing to me for a relationship. I'm still open to it. Throughout my life, my father has asked me for many things, but never forgiveness.

I believe in forgiveness. I give it freely and in doing so, free myself.

YOLANDA YOUNG *is a lawyer in Washington, D.C., and author of the book and syndicated column,* On Our Way to Beautiful. *She previously worked for the National Football League Players' Association. Young is on the board of the PEN/Faulkner Foundation.*

A Potential for Brutality

~

Yinong Young-Xu

I believe in our innate potential for brutality.

When I was six, in the streets of Shanghai, near the end of the Chinese Cultural Revolution, I watched a parade of trucks carrying political dissidents on their way to be publicly executed. At the front of each truck was a young man, roped from head to toe, wearing a sign that said "Counter-revolutionary." If not for that, you would have had trouble guessing what the event was. There was an air of festivity; thousands of bystanders were laughing, talking, gesturing, and pointing at the prisoners. The whole population of Shanghai must have been there. It was like a traditional

Chinese New Year's celebration—except the city was celebrating its own brutality.

I believe that we are brutal because innocence can be corrupted, like mine was as a six-year-old in a time of revolution. When I entered first grade, I started to wave flags, denounce the politically fallen of the day, and shout, "Death to counterrevolutionaries!" My friends and I did not want to miss any of the meetings where political dissidents were publicly tortured and humiliated. That was entertainment for us, just the way movies are for American kids.

Science has taught us that normal genes in cells can be damaged or mutated to become deadly "oncogenes" that result in cancer. I believe brutality is a disease just like cancer; each and every one of us is at risk, including me. I used to fantasize about revenge against the Japanese for the atrocities they committed against the Chinese in World War II. Once I reduced an utterly innocent Japanese girl to tears. I said many cruel things and couldn't stop the venom from pouring out even though I had already begun to feel sorry for her. When our better instincts are suppressed, isn't that the beginning of brutality?

I am fortunate. I was too young to be a Red Guard where my brutality would have been codified. And I had a grandmother who showed me the value of kindness. My own capacity for brutality has never been fully tested. But I believe it is always there.

We're taught not to smoke in order to prevent carcinogens from damaging the genes in our cells. I wish we could learn to prevent hatred from forming and brutality from actualizing. I teach my children that hitting is not allowed, period. I encourage them to be compassionate, to aid those in need, and to stand up for the weak. Most of all, I try to be vigilant over the purity of my motives and cautious about my actions. I believe I must guard against my own potential for brutality and the mutation of my own humanity.

YINONG YOUNG-XU *emigrated from Shanghai to the United States when he was sixteen. He has a doctorate in epidemiology from Harvard, and now researches post-traumatic stress disorder in veterans. Young-Xu visits China to help vaccinate children there against rotavirus.*

A Duty to Family, Heritage, and Country

Ying Ying Yu

I AM A GOOD CHILD, OBEDIENT. I grew up in China, a country where education is the center of every child's life and a grade less than 85 percent is considered a failure. Grades mean more to us than a mother's smile, more than the murmur of a wish lingering on birthday candles. I had homework during lunch, math and language classes two times a day. There were punishments for not paying attention. I was beaten with a ruler. I learned to do anything to get a good grade.

I believe in duty, but that belief comes with sacrifice. The achievements I make come with a cost.

I remember first grade, the red scarf flapping in the wind, wanting more than anything to be the first one to wear it—the symbol of responsibility, excellence, and loyalty. The first thing that flashed to mind when I put it on was how glad my family would be, how proud the motherland would be of the child it had borne, and how my accomplishments would look on a college application.

All my pride, love, self-esteem, they merge into duty. There have been times I wanted to throw away everything, but duty and obligation were always there to haunt me and to keep me strong. I would think: My parents and grandparents brought me up, my country gave me shelter, my teachers spent so much time building my foundations just to have me throw it all away? No, I can't do that! I must repay all that they have done. "I must," "I should," "I have to," all those little phrases govern my life and the lives of many of my classmates. We struggle on because duty reminds us that the awaiting success is not just for us. It's for our families, our heritage, and our country.

I used to want to be a gardener. I liked working outdoors and the gritty feel of dirt was much more tangible than a bunch of flimsy words strung together. But I can never grow up to be a gardener. Everything I have done so far points to the direction of becoming a lawyer. That's a job my family wholeheartedly supports.

There is no other choice for someone who's been brought up by such a strict system, someone who has ambition. Here in America, there is almost a pressure to follow your dreams. I don't want any more dreams—dreams are illusions. And it's too late for me to work toward another future, to let the foundations I have built go to ruins.

I believe in the power of duty to impel. Only duty will offer me something true, something worthy of my effort and the support of my family and country. Duty can bring me to an achievement that is greater than I am.

YING YING YU *was thirteen years old when her social studies class was assigned to write* This I Believe *essays. Yu and her parents immigrated to the United States in 2001. She is a high school student in Princeton Junction, New Jersey.*

We're All Different in Our Own Ways

Joshua Yuchasz

What if everyone in the world was exactly alike? What if everyone talked the same, acted the same, listened to the same music, and watched the same TV programs? The world would be extremely dull!

I believe it's important to accept people for who they are.

Differences are important and they should be respected. For example, many important people throughout history were considered different, such as Thomas Edison, Albert Einstein, Harriet Tubman, Peter Tchaikovsky, and Abraham Lincoln. They did great things, but some people thought they were weird because they had strong feelings about something. I can relate to these people because I've been in that situation before, many times.

It all started in elementary school when I realized that I wasn't like everyone else. My mom says that I have a tendency of obsessing on certain subjects. Unfortunately, these subjects don't interest other kids my age and they really don't interest my teachers. In fact, my kindergarten teacher said she would scream if I mentioned snakes or lizards one more time while she was teaching the days of the week. I would get in trouble for not paying attention—and the teasing began.

In third grade, my teacher informed me that I have Asperger's syndrome. I said, "So what? Do you know that Godzilla's suit weighs one hundred and eighty-eight pounds?"

Later, I asked my mom, "What is Asperger's syndrome? Am I gonna die?" She said that it's like having blinders on, and that I can only see one thing at a time, and that it's hard to focus on other things. Like, I would tell anyone and everyone that would listen about Godzilla because my big obsession was, and still is, Godzilla—not a real popular subject with the middle school crowd, and so the teasing continues.

I might be different, because I have different interests

than other teenagers, but that doesn't give them the right to be so mean and cruel to me. Kids at Oak Valley make fun of me for liking what I like the most.

People also make fun of me for knowing facts about volcanoes, whales, tornadoes, and many other scientific things. My mom says that she has been able to answer many questions on *Jeopardy!* just by listening to what I have to say, but I've even been ridiculed for being smart. Maybe someday, I'll become a gene engineer and create the real Godzilla. I can dream, can't I?

Sometimes I wish I were like everyone else, but not really. Because I believe people should be respected for being different—because we're all different in our own ways. This I believe.

Fourteen-year-old JOSHUA YUCHASZ *was a high school freshman in Milford, Michigan, when he wrote his essay. He plays in his school's concert band and on its football team. In addition to Godzilla, Yuchasz likes other reptiles including Bubba, his pet red-tailed boa constrictor.*

Afterword

~~~

DAN GEDIMAN

IT HAS BEEN BOTH ASTONISHING AND HUMBLING to experience the overwhelming response to our radio series. Since we first debuted on NPR in spring 2005, we have been inundated with calls, letters, and e-mails from people wishing to participate in *This I Believe* in some way. And so what started as a weekly broadcast of three-minute essays about core personal beliefs has turned into a grassroots movement: Tens of thousands of people have accepted our invitation to write their own essays. Others have been interested in organizing *This I Believe* events in their communities. And some just wanted to tell us a story about how *This I Believe* has affected their lives in some way.

The *This I Believe* essay-writing exercise has been used in coffeehouses, adult literacy programs, writers' groups, hospices, hospitals, diversity training, houses of worship, retirement homes, and prisons. Newspapers and public radio stations have been inspired to create their own local versions of our series. And educators across the world have widely embraced *This I Believe* as a writing assignment that asks students to examine their own core beliefs. We have found that the experience of reading, writing, and sharing *This I Believe* essays is transformative, both for individuals and often for their communities.

In Nashville, the staff of Magdalene, a recovery program for women with a criminal history of prostitution and drug addiction, asked their residents to write *This I Believe* statements. With the help of a writing instructor, the women crafted their essays over a period of a few months. In the fall of 2006, Magdalene organizers decided to include these reflections in a fund-raising event for the project. The individual authors presented their essays while a choir of Magdalene women and Grammy Award–winning Nashville singers and songwriters performed "Go Down Moses" as a musical backdrop for the readings.

Magdalene's community relations director, Marlei Olson,

told us, "*This I Believe* gets to the heart of the matter ... and quickly. Our women responded, we responded, because it allows everyone to hit the 'pause' button. For a couple of minutes, you hear the essence of someone's story—the sort of wisdom that only comes from a life deeply lived. *This I Believe* gave them, gives all of us ... the courage to say, 'This is who I am—this I believe about myself, about life, about the world.'"

Another group that has enthusiastically adopted the *This I Believe* essay as a means of self-exploration is educators. An average of twenty-three hundred teachers per month download our free curricula, which have been used in classrooms ranging from elementary to graduate school, and in disciplines including English, speech, communications, social studies, psychology, American studies, history, and even art and band. Of the more than 65,000 essay submissions we have received to date, more than 30 percent have come from young people under the age of eighteen.

Because teachers have found so many creative ways to use our essay-writing project in their classrooms, we created an online forum for educators to share their use of *This I Believe* with one another. This database houses information about how individual educators have been using our project with various age groups and scholastic disciplines. Our hope is that teachers can be inspired by one another and, in turn, help their students find their own source of inspiration.

Susan Carley, who teaches at Buffalo Grove High School in Algonquin, Illinois, told us, "This has been one of the most enriching writing assignments I have ever experienced in my twenty years of teaching. The assignment has been a lesson in taking risks, developing voice, and being concise. As we celebrated finishing our essays—many students choosing to read theirs out loud—our class cried, laughed, and stood in awe of the depth and passion exhibited. Thank you for this experience."

Often these educational activities reach beyond the boundaries of the classroom. At the University of Vermont, for instance, environmental policy professor Cecilia Danks asked her students to write *This I Believe* essays to help them focus their own commitment to the environment. Twenty-one-year-old Michelle Gardner-Quinn wrote a passionate statement encouraging a reverence for all life, especially in the natural world. In her essay, she affirmed her commitment and dedication to helping prevent a worldwide ecological crisis. Two days after submitting her essay, Michelle was abducted and murdered. Yet her essay had a resounding effect: At the Live Earth concerts in July 2007, a video featuring Tipper Gore, Meg Ryan, Sheryl Crow, and Princess of York Sarah Ferguson reading Michelle's essay was shown to an audience of millions. Even after Michelle's death, her words are inspiring others to achieve her goals.

To help more young people get involved in our project, *This I Believe* has created a "For Youth" section on its Web site. These pages include tips for writing and submitting an essay as well as a database of essays submitted to our project by those under eighteen. When asked about their experience of writing a *This I Believe* essay, many students admit that they had to write it for an assignment, though most also admit that they found the experience to be quite enlightening. Ashley, a high school student from Walker, Michigan, told us, "Once I got started, it easily flowed out of my mind and through my hand and onto the paper. I loved this experience. It was amazing to see my thoughts on paper and know that I was pulling down all the walls and barriers to my thoughts for anyone and everyone to see."

A key aspect of *This I Believe* is the sharing of our personal beliefs with one another. We were delighted when our publisher asked if we would consider collecting these essays and making them available in written form. The first volume of *This I Believe* achieved critical acclaim and was a national bestseller, unusual for a collection of essays. We wonder if the success of the book demonstrates a desire—perhaps even a need—for Americans to explore our deeper beliefs, our commonalities, the threads that hold us together.

At many public events held over the past four years to promote the radio series and our first book, we were surprised—and inspired—to see so many people come out to hear readings of essays. Seats were filled, more chairs were brought in, and still there was standing room only. And, yet, when an essayist stepped before the microphone to read his or her own heartfelt words, the crowd listened carefully and attentively. We have learned, again and again, that the power of the *This I Believe* essay goes well beyond the writing down of one's belief. It is the *sharing* and *listening* that provide us opportunities to understand one another and respect beliefs that are different from our own.

We encourage you—and your friends, your family, your neighbors—to explore *This I Believe* together. Visit our Web site, www.thisibelieve.org, to read some of the tens of thousands of statements of belief collected for the project. Search the entries based on city or state, age range, or on a theme or keyword that interests you. E-mail them to friends to start a discussion about their beliefs. Ask your parents or your children to "swap" *This I Believe* essays. Hold book club meetings. Ask your house of worship to involve its members in the sharing of essays. Download and share our middle school, high school, or college curriculum with your teachers or your children's teachers.

We hope that you are inspired after reading this

book—perhaps to write your *own* essay, to organize a *This I Believe* event, or to think of some other idea that will bring *This I Believe* to life in your community. We think you will find that others around you are ready—and eager—for this kind of personal dialogue.

Thom Hawkins, a listener from Berkeley, California, summed it up this way in an e-mail to us: "I see many signs of a pent-up desire throughout our society to emphasize what connects us, rather than what separates us, to focus on commonalities that override our differences. And that is precisely the dominant force behind the *This I Believe* series. It opens our eyes to the values we all share without trivializing our very substantial differences."

How to Write Your Own *This I Believe* Essay

We invite you to contribute to this project by writing and submitting your own statement of personal belief. We understand how challenging this is—it requires intense self-examination, and many find it difficult to begin. To guide you through this process, we offer these suggestions:

Tell a story: Be specific. Take your belief out of the ether and ground it in the events of your life. Your story need not be heartwarming or gut-wrenching—it can even be funny—but it should be *real*. Consider moments when your belief was formed, tested, or changed. Make sure your story ties to the essence of your daily life philosophy and to the shaping of your beliefs.

Be brief: Your statement should be between 350 and 500 words. The shorter length forces you to focus on the belief that is central to your life.

Name your belief: If you can't name it in a sentence or two, your essay might not be about belief. Rather than writing a list, consider focusing on one core belief.

Be affirmative: Say what you do believe, not what you don't believe. Avoid statements of religious dogma, preaching, or editorializing.

Be personal: Make your essay about you; speak in the first person. Try reading your essay aloud to yourself several times, and each time edit it and simplify it until you find the words, tone, and story that truly echo your belief and the way you speak.

Please submit your completed essay to the *This I Believe* project, by visiting the Web site, www.thisibelieve.org.

APPENDIX B

How to Use *This I Believe* in Your Community

This I Believe is a national project that provides your community exciting opportunities to strengthen civic discourse that is honest and respectful, authentic and intimate, through writing and sharing short statements of personal belief.

We hope to inspire you to reflect, encourage you to share, and engage you in a conversation about personal values and beliefs that can shape your life, your community, and our society.

And writing a *This I Believe* essay is just the first step.

We encourage you to come together with friends,

neighbors, and acquaintances to discuss in a respectful manner the essays you've read or written—in the classroom, in public spaces, and in places of worship. To help you do this in your community, we offer these tools, which are available on our Web site, www.thisibelieve.org:

HANDBOOK FOR COMMUNITY EVENT COORDINATORS

By working with communities around the country, we hope to create real and virtual spaces where citizens can come together to discuss the core values that guide our daily lives. To accomplish this goal, we want to take the conversation beyond the airwaves and bring it to your community. This handbook presents a number of suggestions that you can execute in order to promote and stage events to engage your community in a *This I Believe* event.

EDUCATIONAL CURRICULA

This I Believe currently provides three downloadable curricula, one suitable for use in middle schools, one for high schools, and the third for colleges and universities. These educational curricula were designed to help teachers guide students in the writing of a *This I Believe* essay. The curricular exercises help students understand the concept of belief, explore their own values, and then craft a well-written essay.

DISCUSSION GUIDES

We have produced a general discussion guide to help you engage a group in a moderated conversation about belief and values. It is appropriate for use in classrooms, civic clubs, libraries, senior centers, coffeehouses, and other public venues. There is also a specifically tailored guide for use in houses of worship. Both guides include ground rules for structuring dialogue to ensure thought-provoking conversations, and tips for writing and sharing essays.

POSTER AND BROCHURE

We have designed print materials to help you spread the word about *This I Believe* activities happening in your community. Download a free poster or brochure that may be customized with specific details.

To download these resources, read additional information about the series, or contact the project team, please visit the Web site www.thisibelieve.org.

Acknowledgments

We offer our deepest thanks to the essayists who contributed their personal statements to this book. We honor their willingness to explore and express the things that matter most.

In reviving this series we owe a debt to Casey Murrow, Keith Wheelock, and Margot Wheelock Schlegel, the children of *This I Believe* founders Edward R. Murrow and Ward Wheelock. Our radio series on NPR was guided by Edward R. Murrow and his team that preceded us in the 1950s: Gladys Chang Hardy, Reny Hill, Donald J. Merwin, Edward P. Morgan, Raymond Swing, and Ward Wheelock.

Some of the essays in this volume were shepherded by our colleagues Emily Botein and Ellen Silva, and we are indebted to them for their contribution. Our thanks as well to Mary Jo Gediman, who has been invaluable in preparing the manuscript of this book.

Our office staff at This I Believe, Inc., particularly our office managers, Anetta Shaw and Kelly Skinner, have provided limitless enthusiasm and energy in keeping us on track throughout the process of creating this book and the radio series. We are especially grateful to Georg Brandl Egloff for creating our elegant theme music.

Our production partner for the broadcasts on NPR was Atlantic Public Media, Inc., in Woods Hole, Massachusetts, where all the essay submissions were reviewed by a dedicated group of readers, including Samantha Broun, Sydney Lewis, Chelsea Merz, Melissa Robbins, Helen Woodward, and Sarah Yahm. We thank the Cape and Islands public radio stations WCAI, WNAN, and WZAI, and their parent station WGBH, for providing a home for that team.

For their advice and assistance, we acknowledge our This I Believe, Inc., Board of Directors: Stuart Adams, Vaughn Bell, John Y. Brown, III, Sean Heitkemper, Jim Higgins, and Michael Shields.

Many in NPR's news division helped guide the series

along the way, particularly the staffs of *All Things Considered*, *Weekend Edition Sunday*, and *Morning Edition*, including Davar Ardalan, Bruce Auster, Jenni Bergal, Melissa Block, Greg Dixon, Brian Duffy, Susan Feeney, Sue Goodwin, Liane Hansen, Jeremy Hobson, Steve Inskeep, Bob Malesky, Ellen McDonnell, Maeve McGoren, Sarah Mobley, Renee Montagne, Michele Norris, David Rector, Robert Siegel, Christopher Turpin, and Ellen Weiss. We are grateful to Jay Kernis who was a steady champion for the idea of reviving Murrow's series on public radio.

The Web site for *This I Believe* was built by Toni Steinhauer, Dennis Whiteman, and Leap Frog Interactive, and we are grateful for their talents in helping us make all the essays submitted to our project available for everyone to read. In addition, for their fine work, we thank the staff at NPR Digital Media, including: Michael Horn, Michael Katzif, Melody Kokoszka, Joe Matazzoni, Bryan Moffet, Beth Novey, Christina Nunez, Robert Spier, Maria Thomas, and Michael Yoch.

NPR also provided administrative support for our series—technical production, underwriting and promotion, station services, business development, and countless other ways—with strong guidance from Stacey Foxwell. Our thanks go to Julia Bailey, Carlos Barrionuevo, Anna Christopher,

Jacques Coughlin, Bill Craven, Michael Cullen, Katie Daugert, Scott Davis, Kitty Eisele, Alyne Ellis, Meghan Gallery, Micah Greenberg, Penny Hain, Barbara Hall, Neal Jackson, Jane Kelly, Kevin Klose, Richard Knox, Vanessa Krabacher, Jenny Lawhorn, Denise Leary, Jeeun Lee, Joyce MacDonald, Kathie Miller, Laura Mirsch, Jeff Nemic, Meredith Olsen, Ben Rogot, Marty Ronish, Barbara Sopato, Andi Sporkin, Ken Stern, Neil Tevault, Blake Truitt, Derek Turner, John Verdi, Barbara Vierow, and Roger Wight.

Two essays in this book are a result of our collaboration with the Canadian Broadcasting Corporation, which produced its own *This I Believe* radio series in 2007. We thank Barbara Brown, Linda Groen, Judy McAlpine, and producer Anne Penman for their stewardship of the *This I Believe* series in Canada.

Without our funders, our radio series would not have been possible. *This I Believe* received the first faithful leap of funding from the Corporation for Public Broadcasting. Our thanks go to the able staff of CPB's radio and grants divisions, including Deborah Carr and Kathy Merritt. Our second year of broadcast was generously underwritten by Capella University. Our third and fourth years were underwritten by Prudential Retirement. Our most sincere thanks to Jim Mallozzi and Dean Houldcroft at Prudential for being such stalwart friends of *This I Believe*. The balance of our budget was provided by The Righteous Persons Foundation and by the Prudential Foundation.

We are also appreciative of the myriad educators who have helped us reach beyond the broadcast into classrooms to inspire today's youth to consider and write about their beliefs. We are indebted to Dottie Willis for writing our high school curriculum, Dr. Kyle Dickson and Dr. Cole Bennett for authoring our college curriculum, and Amanda Cadran for creating our middle school curriculum.

The creation of this book was ably guided by our agent Lynn Nesbit and her associates at Janklow & Nesbit, including Tina Simms, Cullen Stanley, and particularly Bennett Ashley.

Our publisher, Henry Holt and Company, has been supportive through both volumes of *This I Believe*. We thank Dan Farley, John Sterling, and our enthusiastic editor David Patterson. Also at Holt and their sister company Macmillan Audio, we are grateful to Emily Belford, Patrick Clark, Devin Coats, Barbara Cohen, Denise Cronin, Flora Easterly, Lisa Fyfe, Justin Golenbock, Margo Goody, Donna Holstein, Jeanne-Marie Hudson, Christine Kopprasch, Eileen Lawrence, Meryl Levavi, Jason Liebman, Kelly Lignos, Claire McKinney, Rita Quintas, Richard Rhorer, Maggie Richards, Tammy Richards, Mary Beth Roche, Kenn Russell, Bob Van Kolken, and Laura Wilson.

And, finally, we thank the thousands of individuals who have accepted our invitation to write and share their own personal statements of belief. This book contains but a fraction of the many thoughtful and inspiring essays that have been submitted to our project, and we are grateful for them all.

—JAY ALLISON, DAN GEDIMAN, JOHN GREGORY, AND VIKI MERRICK

About the Editors

JAY ALLISON, the curator and producer of the *This I Believe* radio series on NPR, is an independent broadcast journalist. His work appears often on NPR's *All Things Considered* and *Morning Edition* and PRI's *This American Life*, and he has earned five Peabody Awards. His essays have appeared in *The New York Times Magazine* and other publications. He is cocreator of Transom.org, which gives people the tools to tell their own stories, and of the Public Radio Exchange (prx.org), which helps get those stories on the air. Allison is the founder of the public radio stations that serve Martha's Vineyard, Nantucket, and Cape Cod, where he lives.

DAN GEDIMAN is the executive producer of *This I Believe*. His work has been heard on *All Things Considered*, *Morning Edition*,

Fresh Air, Marketplace, Soundprint, Jazz Profiles, and *This American Life.* During his twenty-year radio career, Gediman has won many of public broadcasting's most prestigious awards for programs such as *Breaking the Cycle: How Do We Stop Child Abuse?* and *I Just Am Who We Are: A Portrait of Multiple Personality Disorder.* He also worked with legendary radio playwright Norman Corwin to produce *13 by Corwin* and *50 Years After 14 August,* which won the duPont-Columbia Award.

FROM THE EDITORS

One of our goals with this project is to compile as complete an archive as possible of Edward R. Murrow's 1950s series. You may be able to help us with this task. If you possess any materials relating to *This I Believe,* be they recordings, newspaper or magazine clippings, essays written by yourself or a family member (perhaps a school assignment that you have kept over the years), or correspondence with the *This I Believe* staff, we would love to have a copy for our archive. Thank you in advance for your help.

This I Believe, Inc.
P.O. Box 5031
Louisville, KY 40255-0031

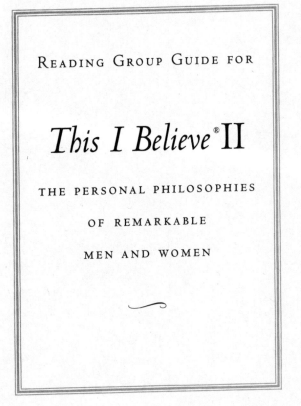

READING GROUP GUIDE FOR

This I Believe®II

THE PERSONAL PHILOSOPHIES

OF REMARKABLE

MEN AND WOMEN

Discussion Questions

1. Dramatic events such as Hurricane Katrina and the Iraq War are topics in many of these essays. How, if at all, have recent events shaped your beliefs?

2. Belief in mankind is a common theme among Ernesto Haibi, Roald Hoffmann, and many more. What are some of the recurring threads in these essays? What are their differences? How do these essays stand in light of Yinong Young-Xu's "A Potential for Brutality"? Can these views be reconciled?

3. Tony Hawk, a skateboarder, Yolanda O'Bannon, a secretary, and Dan Tani, an astronaut, write about doing what they love. What does it take to follow one's own path? What sacrifices are required? What would you be doing, if you could?

4. Several of the essays discuss the role music can play in discovering belief, such as Bela Fleck's thoughts on figuring out his own way to do things, Yo-Yo Ma's observations on exploring cultures and traditions, and Joan Tower's view on the power of music. Why do you think music can be such a powerful tool in determining beliefs?

5. Susan Cooke Kittredge writes, "I believe in mending." Do we all need mending? She is starting with her pajamas. Where would you start?

6. Laura Shipler Chico discussed the three qualities she'd like her child to have. What three qualities would you choose for a child? How about for yourself or a mate?

7. Robin Baudier and Andy Blowers turned adversity into what Baudier calls "strange blessings." Is there

anything in your own life that could be called a strange blessing?

8. David Buetow believes in his dog. How does looking beyond the human—to animals, things, and places—influence the way we believe or behave?

9. Among the vastly different views on marriage in the world are Corinne Colbert's belief that her husband is "good enough" and Betsy Chalmers's perspective of loyalty to an incarcerated spouse. Are there any universal truths about marriage?

10. This book includes essays from students, as well as essays on growing old. What differences or similarities do you find between these age-specific essays, if any?

11. Do you agree with Sister Helen Prejean, that what we do is what we believe? If so, would you want to change anything you do to better match your beliefs? Do you think that most people would be proud to claim their actions as beliefs?

12. If peace begins with one person, as Ivory Harlow believes, how can each of us contribute? Do any of these essays inspire you to action?

13. What do you believe? What were your greatest influences in shaping those beliefs? How have your beliefs changed throughout your life?

14. Has there been someone in your life who instilled your beliefs in you or inspired you in that way?

15. Is there a time when your core beliefs were shaken or tested, perhaps in ways that were uncomfortable or dangerous?